What to buy for your baby

What to buy for your baby

Choosing the right equipment for you

Liat Hughes Joshi and Caroline Cosgrove

Viva Books
New Delhi | Mumbai | Chennai | Kolkata
Bangalore | Hyderabad | Kochi | Guwahati

First Indian Edition 2010

VIVA BOOKS PRIVATE LIMITED

- 4737/23 Ansari Road, Daryaganj, New Delhi 110 002
  E-mail: vivadelhi@vivagroupindia.net, Tel. 42242200
- 76, Service Industries, Shirvane, Sector 1, Nerul, Navi Mumbai 400 706
  E-mail: vivamumbai@vivagroupindia.net, Tel. 27721273, 27721274
- Jamals Fazal Chambers, 26 Greams Road, Chennai 600 006
  E-mail: vivachennai@vivagroupindia.net, Tel. 28290304, 28294241
- B-103, Jindal Towers, 21/1A/3 Darga Road, Kolkata 700 017
  E-mail: vivakolkata@vivagroupindia.net, Tel. 22836381, 22816713
- 7, Sovereign Park Apartments, 56-58, K. R. Road, Basavanagudi, Bangalore 560 004
  E-mail: vivabangalore@vivagroupindia.net, Tel. 26607409, 26607410
- 101-102 Mughal Marc Apartments, 3-4-637 to 641, Narayanguda, Hyderabad 500 029
  E-mail: vivahyderabad@vivagroupindia.net, Tel. 27564481, 27564482
- Beevi Towers, First Floor, SRM Road, Kaloor, Kochi 682 018, Kerala
  E-mail: vivakochi@vivagroupindia.net, Tel: 0484-2403055, 2403056
- 232, GNB Road, Beside UCO Bank, Silpukhuri, Guwahati 781 003
  E-mail: vivaguwahati@vivagroupindia.net, Tel: 0361-2666386

www.vivagroupindia.com

Published by arrangement with

Crimson Publishing,
a division of Crimson Business Ltd
Westminster House, Kew Road
Richmond, Surrey TW9 2ND

ISBN : 978-81-309-1488-6

Published by Vinod Vasishtha for Viva Books Private Limited, 4737/23, Ansari Road, Daryaganj, New Delhi - 110 002.

Printed and bound by Raj Press, R-3, Inderpuri, New Delhi - 110 012.

ACKNOWLEDGEMENTS

Thanks to our 'parent panel' especially Niyati Keni, Tracey Harper, Carl Smith, Julia Nicholson, Catriona Hughes, Sarah Wild, Karen Hughes, Tanya Steenson, Derek Ross, Jennefer Khan, Sue Breeze, and Karol-ann Hewgill. Thanks also to breastfeeding expert Geraldine Miskin and Chris May, our car seat 'guru'.

To our husbands, Dhaval and Nick, for enduring endless discussions of baby products.

And to our children, Luca, Juliette and James, for inadvertently getting us started with this whole baby gear thing in the first place.

ABOUT THE AUTHORS

Liat Hughes Joshi is a freelance journalist who has contributed to the parenting magazine Junior, *The Sunday Times*, *The Independent on Sunday*, and *The Guardian*. She has in-depth knowledge of baby products and has written numerous product tests and reviews. She lives in North London with her husband and son.

Caroline Cosgrove established Baby Concierge, the nursery advisory service, in 2002. Since then she has advised parents-to-be from all walks of life on every aspect of baby shopping. Unlike a conventional shop, Baby Concierge is wholly independent, advising clients solely according to their needs, and with no affiliation to specific manufacturers or products. Caroline recently co-founded **www.babyfy.com**, an information website that, uniquely, profiles and reviews both baby products and UK maternity units. She has two children and also lives in North London.

Contents

Introduction

THANK GOODNESS FOR THE NINE MONTHS' NOTICE

You've got what seem like a million and one things to buy for a person you've never even met. Everyone's offering conflicting advice – one friend swears by her fancy nappy disposal bin with its deodorising refill cartridges, another thinks they're an insane waste of money. One friend waxes lyrical about baby slings, another just couldn't get the hang of hers.

Advice on the internet is no more definitive and who knows whether that shop assistant has your best interests or their sales figures at heart.

Welcome to the world of baby shopping. It's crammed with products designed to tempt you to part with your cash and the amount of choice out there can be thoroughly overwhelming. You're going to encounter items you probably didn't even know existed before conceiving and sometimes you'll wish you had a special 'baby kit' dictionary to decipher the terminology. Take prams: there are two-in-ones, three-in-ones, travel systems, three-wheelers, buggies, umbrella folders, telescopic folders. It's almost enough to bring on early labour.

Want to know the pros and cons of microwave, cold water or steam sterilisers or whether it's best to go for cherry-shaped or orthodontic soothers? Want to know how many sleepsuits to buy and in what size, or what to consider when choosing a car seat?

Well, think of us as your own personal shoppers, guiding you impartially through the jungle of baby kit and easing some of the stress of preparing for your newborn's arrival.

We'll let you know which items are essential, which are optional and which, in our view, will more than likely gather dust. Where there are choices (and believe us there are many) we discuss the pros and cons of the main options. Although we mention our favourite brands and specific products this is not our main focus – products change too quickly and there are too many to cover here anyway. When we do recommend particular brands, you can be assured we're entirely independent with no vested interests.

We've included shopping lists at the start of each chapter and a complete list at the end of the book, and provided details of useful websites. Throughout the book you'll also find eco-friendly tips and general advice.

Baby gear can be surprisingly controversial and many choices are quite personal – not everyone will agree with everything we say (feel free to email us your views at **comments@whattobuyforyourbaby.co.uk**). But we've consulted far and wide and assembled our very own 'parent panel' – a group of knowledgeable parents who've been there, done that and have the bags under their eyes to show for it. We've put their views together with our own extensive experience of baby products – both professional and as mothers, to provide you with all the information you need to make decisions.

We hope that by using this book, 'baby shopping' will be fun and stress-free rather than the chore it can easily become. Perhaps with our help you can spend a little less time waddling around nursery shops and a little more time resting those swollen ankles and supping a nice cup of decaf.

SOME PRACTICALITIES

When to start

When to begin shopping for baby things is a question we often get asked – we recommend starting some time after the 20-week scan. By then you'll probably be mentally ready to prepare for the baby's arrival but you'll still have plenty of time for deliberation. Don't leave it all too late as some items have long lead times, or might be out of stock, and of course babies can arrive early.

Some religions and cultures prefer parents-to-be to delay purchases until after the birth. If this applies to you, do as much 'window shopping' and planning as possible and then get a friend or relative to collect everything whilst you're in hospital. Or use the 'delayed delivery' services offered by some retailers, where you select items in advance but only pay and receive them after the birth.

If you don't know the baby's sex

If you don't know whether you'll be hearing 'it's a boy' or 'it's a girl' at the birth, consider these options when shopping:

- *buy everything but choose neutral items that work for both genders.*
- *buy neutral essentials and then wait until after the birth for everything else.*
- *buy both boyish and girly things from shops where they can be returned or exchanged.*

If you intend to have more children later on, it's wise to go with gender-neutral choices for major items anyway – a pink pram or ballerina-embellished furniture might be lovely for a girl but what if she's joined by a younger brother one day and you want to reuse these things?

Help I'm having more than one!

If you're expecting twins or more, baby shopping brings a few extra challenges and certainly extra costs. On the whole the decisions you need to make will be similar to those for just one baby but where there are special considerations, we've included 'twin tips'. For further advice on preparing for twins check out the Twins and Multiple Births Association's website [**www.tamba.org.uk**].

How much is this going to cost?

There's no simple answer. It depends on your financial situation, whether you're a designer label fan or a thrifty type (by choice or necessity) and how much you want to borrow or buy second-hand.

According to one survey, the *average* parents-to-be spent a daunting £1,060 on baby stuff before the birth. One in seven spent between £2,000 and £2,500 and a few coughed up a staggering £5,800 plus.

There truly is no need to spend so much – eBay, NCT nearly new sales and friends are all excellent sources of second-hand kit. In the relevant chapters, we cover which items are well suited to second-hand purchase or borrowing from friends or family, and what to look out for when doing so, as safety standards may have changed since items were originally bought.

Whether you're after a bargain, some luxuries or just practical advice, we're here to help. Happy shopping!

Key to symbols:

Our star buys for each product category. If none are listed it's because products of that type are fairly similar or we don't recommend buying in that category anyway. A star buy won't necessarily be cheap but it will, in our opinion, offer good value for what it is and be amongst the best of its type at the time of writing.

££ Money-saving tips – these include recommendations for multi-functional items you'll get stacks of use out of, cheap and cheerful products that do the job just as well as pricier alternatives, and good old-fashioned advice that can help you cut down on spending.

eco-friendly products and tips.

Advice for those expecting twins (or more).

Safety alert – information and advice to help keep your baby safe.

You'll also see the following symbols in our shopping lists:

✓ indicates an essential. Occasionally this refers to something that you could in theory manage without but which we thoroughly recommend to make life easier.

? – optional buys – useful or helpful items but you can certainly live without them.

✗ – things we think aren't worth wasting money on. There will always be someone who disagrees, but on the whole we think it's best to leave such items on the nursery shop's shelves.

1

Pre-birth essentials

This is the stuff you absolutely need to have ready *before* the birth. Other items listed as essential in the book won't be needed the day you get home from hospital (although you might choose to have them ready before the birth anyway). For more information and quantities see the relevant chapters.

- Appropriate sleeping place (Moses basket/carrycot/crib/hammock or cot)
- Bedding for the above (mattress protector, sheets and blankets)
- Group 0+ car seat
- Changing bag or equivalent
- Nipple cream and breast pads
- Baby bottles, formula and steriliser if you intend to bottle-feed from birth
- Clothing basics (newborn hats, bodysuits, sleepsuits, scratch mitts, socks, cardigans, bibs)
- Nappies (plus a pail for storage if using washables)
- Nappy sacks
- Cotton wool
- Soft towel solely for your baby's use
- Muslin squares

THE BEST
OUR PERSONAL FAVOURITE BABY PRODUCTS

We couldn't resist telling you about the products that we absolutely love and which we've tried and tested on our own children.

Liat's top products

- Ergo Baby Carrier – comfortable for wearer and child well into the toddler phase, packs small, and many kids love the piggyback-like back position.
- Bedside crib – one side drops totally away so you can sleep right beside your baby and reach out to hold their tiny hand without the worries of bed-sharing.
- Disposable changing mats – not terribly eco-friendly but each can be reused lots of times and if you do encounter a particularly grubby changing table when out, you *can* throw them away rather than worrying about your lovely one getting another baby's germs (or worse) on it.
- Frozen fresh baby food such as Babylicious and Truly Scrumptious – if you aren't keen on the idea of jarred baby food, this is a hassle-free and additive-free alternative to cooking your own.
- Sudocrem – not just for nappy rash but a whole host of other things like noses sore from a cold.

Caroline's top products

- Tripp Trapp highchair – the philosophy of this highchair is that your child benefits from being included at the family table. It's also a great investment as it can be adapted for use from six months to old age and is stylish and comfy to boot.
- Hug-a-bub – this wrap sling holds your baby secure and close and

distributes the weight so well that you can 'wear your baby' for long stretches in comfort.

- My Brest Friend – correct positioning is key to successful breastfeeding and this breastfeeding pillow is the best for helping you get that right, whilst also providing much-needed lower back support.
- A warm mist humidifier – soothes coughs, eases breathing and aids sleep when a baby/child/adult is congested or under the weather.
- Kiddyguard – these stair safety gates practically disappear when not in use, so can be left in place even when your own child is past needing them, meaning they're always on standby should friends with babies visit.

AND THE WORST

Our parent panel fairly consistently said these things were, in retrospect, a waste of money and we tend to agree. Some of these items have their fans but overall, think twice before coughing up for them.

- Especially heavy 'newborn' prams (they usually get traded in for something lighter once the baby hits six months and can sit upright in a buggy).
- 'Starter sets' (bundled products typically for bathing or childproofing – poor value because you probably won't want or need half the stuff).
- Bottle warmer (if your baby won't accept room temperature milk, just place bottles in hot water from the kettle/a flask).
- Bumbo baby seat (not useful for long and if used for feeding you'll have to crouch on the floor as they can't be used on raised surfaces. Worth borrowing though).
- Newborn-sized baby bottles (too small within weeks).
- Home baby weighing scales (go to the health visitor or use your bathroom scales).

- Shopping trolley seat covers (you can always give the seat a wipe).
- Bath rings (difficult to get babies in and out of).

LESS OBVIOUS LIFESAVERS

None of these are baby products per se but they can all be a blessing in disguise during those hectic post-natal weeks.

- Takeaway menus (for when you can't face cooking).
- Supermarket online shopping services (for when you can't face shopping).
- Cordless phone (for when you're pinned down by a feeding/sleeping baby).
- Post-it notes (for when you're too tired to remember anything).
- Microwave (for re-heating baby food).
- Earplugs and eye mask (for extra zzzs during those daytime 'sleep when your baby sleeps' naps).
- Dimmer light switch (for night feeds).
- Stain remover (for when carrot purée gets everywhere).
- A variety of batteries (for your baby's electronic toys).

PARENTING WEBSITES WORTH BOOKMARKING

- **Mumsnet.co.uk** – lively chatroom site where you can find opinions on anything and everything baby-related. Wonderful for seeking advice from experienced parents.
- **Fsid.org** – up-to-date guidance on cot death prevention.
- **Tamba.org.uk** – support and information for those expecting twins or more.
- **Babyfy.com** – profiles and reviews of most baby products on the market, as well as UK hospital maternity units.

- **Nct.org.uk** – information on NCT antenatal and postnatal groups plus nearly new sales.
- **Babycentre.co.uk** – a mine of information on infant and toddler health and development.
- **Letsbreastfeed.com** – breastfeeding help and advice from expert Geraldine Miskin.

SHOPPING WEBSITES TO BOOKMARK

- **Ebay.co.uk** – not just a site for second-hand and unwanted items, retailers offload overstocks of new baby products at amazing prices.
- **Greenbaby.co.uk** – eco-friendly and natural baby products.
- **Babyconcierge.co.uk** – for an idea of what's rated as well as more unusual products you won't find everywhere.
- **Kiddicare.com** – mainstream brands at discounted prices.
- **Bloomingmarvellous.co.uk** and **Jojomamanbebe.co.uk** – mail order/online baby gear shopping
- **Mothercare.com** and **Babiesrus.co.uk** – both offer well-priced own brand products.
- **Johnlewis.com** – a wide selection of good quality nursery products.
- **Ikea.com** – basic, practical baby gear – some serious bargains.

2

Clothing

Shopping list

✓ Sleepsuits (6 x newborn size, 6 x 0-3 months)

✓ Short-sleeved bodysuits (6-8 x newborn, 6-8 x 0-3 months)

✓ 2 cardigans in 0-3 months (lightweight for summer, medium-weight for winter)

✓ 2 hats

✓ 4 pairs of socks

✓ 2 pairs of scratch mitts

✓ 2-3 bibs

✓ 2 pairs of mittens (winter babies only)

? 2-3 sleepgowns

Browsing through rails of utterly adorable little baby clothes can melt the heart of even the least clucky parent-to-be. Cravings for these tiny outfits can be as strong as any for gherkins or pineapple pizza. But it's all too easy to end up with a wardrobe full of barely used baby clothes, so before you head to that shop till, arms piled high, consider a couple of things.

First up, you'll almost certainly get stacks of clothes as presents. When we had our babies we were surprised and touched by the generosity of people we barely knew. OK, a few of the gifts were truly hideous (the hand-knitted, misshapen, lurid orange dungarees received by one of us were 'interesting'), some utterly inappropriate for the season (a newborn size snowsuit for a July baby?) but many of the gifts were lovely.

Secondly, new babies grow very quickly and that tremendously tempting designer outfit might literally get one or two wears before it's stretching at the seams. If you calculate the cost-per-wear, well, it gets scary.

We know ourselves how hard it is to resist purchasing at least a few gorgeous outfits, so go ahead (it's part of the fun of preparing for a baby), but beyond that, try and stick to basics and see what gifts you get before buying half of Baby Gap.

Look for:

- *Washability* – if it can't be machine-washed and tumble-dried, walk away! That pure cashmere baby cardigan *will* get puked on and hand-washing/trips to the dry cleaners are chores you won't welcome in the newborn weeks.

- *Comfort* – it can seem that your mission as a new parent is to do almost anything to minimise your baby's crying – avoiding uncomfortable clothes is one small tactic in this battle against tears. Luckily you don't have to choose between comfort and style as there are some beautiful *and* comfy baby clothes around. Woven or jersey cotton and softest, thin denim are breathable and gentle against sensitive skin.

- Clothes that are *easy to put on and take off* – many babies dislike having clothes pulled over their heads and some parents feel a bit nervous about dressing their newborn, so look for tops with envelope necks, poppered necks that open up wider or wrap-over styles. Cardigans are better than sweaters, and faced with a wriggly baby, poppers and zips are easier to do up than buttons.

- *Easy nappy access* – nappy changing will be a key activity of your day, so go for easy to remove trousers with poppers down the legs and save girls' tights until they're older.
- Shops with a *good returns policy*. Nursery and baby clothing retailers tend to be generous with this and provided something is unworn, many will exchange or give vouchers even if you don't have a receipt. If you do have the receipt, some retailers will take things back long after they were purchased. So retain receipts, leave tags on until you know for sure you want to keep an item and don't rush into washing non-essentials before the birth.

Steer clear of:

- *Clothes that could irritate* your baby. This means avoiding big buttons, itchy lace, and scratchy labels or seams. Check the underside of appliquéd decorations, skip collared shirts that come high up the neck, anything that does up at the back (hard to reach when your baby can't sit up and potentially uncomfortable if they're lying on the seam) and polyester (it can be clammy and irritating to delicate baby skin).
- *Buying lots in newborn/'1 month' size.* Unless you have a particularly small baby, these sizes will only fit for a few weeks. The average newborn weighs about 7lb 11oz at birth, reaching around 10lbs by four weeks. Such clothes might not fit at all if you have an especially bruising baby. Buying a few newborn-sized essentials and then mainly sticking to 0 to 3 months is more economical, although it might mean slightly baggy clothes for the first few weeks.

- *'Starter' sets* of assorted clothing items – you'll probably dislike or won't need some of them. Not the good value they can appear to be.
- *Snowsuits* – quilted all-in-ones look cosy but are impractical – as soon as you've struggled to put them on, sod's law says your baby's nappy will need changing and you'll have to take the whole thing off again! It's also easy for babies to overheat in these, especially if you're going in and out of shops, restaurants, and the car. Since newborns don't tend to go running around in the snow, blankets, pram foot-muffs (see page 134) and 'shaped wraps' are more versatile ways to keep them warm, given these can be easily removed or opened up when you go indoors.
- Expensive baby shoes, hats, gloves and mittens: all are prone to getting lost.

Baby clothing brands we like:

£ *Tesco, H&M, Adams*

££ *Gap, M&S, Zara, Next*

£££ *Timberland, Petit Bateau.*

What the heck's a layette? Some retailers use this mysterious term and sell 'layette' gift sets. Sometimes it means just clothing, sometimes it includes bedding and sometimes bath towels as well.

Organic clothes are increasingly available from mainstream as well as specialist retailers. There's little firm evidence to suggest pesticides or non-organic cottons are terribly harmful to babies but if you prefer to reduce any risk, by all means go organic. A bonus is that organic cotton usually feels extra soft and tends not to be that much more expensive than good quality standard cotton.

NEWBORN ESSENTIALS

Sleepsuits – (also called babygros) these are long-sleeved all-in-one outfits, typically made from stretchy jersey cotton and can form a mainstay for day as well as night wear in the first weeks. They're comfortable, cosy and needn't be pulled over the baby's floppy head. Those with integral 'feet' remove worries about socks dropping off – baby socks are notorious for this and also getting lost in washing machines (sleepsuits with integral scratch mitts are practical for the same reason).

Buy six newborn-size cotton jersey sleepsuits (you could skip the newborn ones if you're expecting a big baby or don't mind them having slightly baggy clothing) and six in 0 to 3 months. Choose sleepsuits that do up with poppers down the front or side and the crotch/legs, and with integral 'feet'. Most department stores and large supermarkets offer reasonably priced multipacks.

Sleepgowns – a practical alternative to sleepsuits for night-time. Sleepgowns are like long nighties which cover the baby's legs and feet. They make night nappy changes easier because there's no fiddling with sleepsuit press studs, you just push the gown above the baby's waist and change away. They can be used under blankets or sleeping bags and as they're looser and don't have integral 'feet', are outgrown less quickly than sleepsuits. Some have integral scratch mitts. On the downside, they have to go over a baby's head when being put on/taken off and some people worry little feet get chilly in them (you can always use socks). Buy one or two initially and see if you prefer them to sleepsuits for nightwear before buying more.

Bodysuits (also called vests) – short or long-sleeved tops that fasten at the crotch with poppers. They'll probably form a mainstay of your baby's wardrobe, worn under another top in cooler weather, or alone in warmer months instead of standard T-shirts. They help keep nappies in place and don't ride up the way normal tops do. If you're worried about pulling things over your baby's head, go for the wrap or 'kimono' style that fasten at the side as well as underneath. Otherwise just ensure the necks are wide 'envelope' ones or very stretchy. Buy six to eight newborn and/or 0 to 3 months in stretch cotton jersey. Again, department stores and supermarkets sell good value multipacks.

Cardigans – choose cotton rather than wool, and poppers or concealed zips rather than tiny buttons which can be annoyingly fiddly. Buy two or three cotton cardigans or hooded tops.

Hand-knits – if a kind friend or relative offers to knit something for your baby, you might worry about landing a dated woolly monstrosity that you can't bear to dress your child in. But hand knits *can* be lovely – if you can do so diplomatically, steer the knitter towards the likes of Debbie Bliss's modern patterns and soft wools [**www.debbieblissonline.com**].

Socks – most baby socks are impossible to keep on. We might sound like an advert for Baby Gap but theirs really are the only ones which we've found reliably stay put. They also have non-slip soles so older, walking babies are less likely to slip on hard floors. If you do end up with a falling-off-socks problem, 'Sock-ons' could help. They're inexpensive little elasticated straps that sit around the heel and instep [see **www.sockons.co.uk**].

Buy four pairs of Baby Gap socks – if you want to be really practical buy them all in one colour, so that if some get lost the remainders make pairs. (That suggestion is firm evidence that we've so turned into our own mothers since having kids …)

Hats and gloves – hats shield your baby from harmful rays in summer and retain body heat in winter (babies haven't much hair to do the latter). Both winter and summer hats should be made from breathable fabrics such as cotton. Avoid brims that go all the way round for newborns who spend most of their time lying on their backs. Legionnaires' hats with back and side flaps offer extra protection for older babies.

Mittens are preferable to gloves as they're easier to put on tiny hands. Buy two hats appropriate to the season and for winter, two pairs of mittens.

Scratch mittens – tiny cotton mittens to stop newborns scratching themselves with their sharp nails. Baby fingernails grow quickly and are tricky to cut, so if you have a 'scratchy' baby, these mitts are essential. Be warned they have a tendency to get lost as they're so titchy. Look out for sleepsuits and sleepgowns with integral ones.

If you need to buy them separately, buy two pairs, then see if your baby is a scratcher before buying more.

OTHER CLOTHING

For special occasions or when you get sick of the sight of sleepsuits, it's time to get some of those more interesting 'proper outfits' out of the wardrobe.

Trousers and shorts – choose any style but remember the usual guidance on practicality and comfort. Soft jersey tracksuit bottoms and shorts are convenient as they're comfy enough to stay on for daytime naps. Go for poppered access to the nappy area or elasticated waists that are easy to pull up and down. If your baby is slimmer than average look for adjustable waistbands.

These aren't essential for a newborn – they'll be fine in sleepsuits, but for older babies, buy four to six pairs (fewer for girls with dresses/skirts, more for both sexes when potty training).

Dresses and skirts – cool and pretty for girls in summer (and super-easy for nappy changing) but not so practical in winter (getting tights onto babies is challenging). Unnecessary for newborns so either just buy a couple for special occasions or wait until your little girl is older – trousers or leggings make better everyday winter wear.

T-shirts – for younger babies, we favour bodysuits instead of T-shirts as the latter tend to ride up exposing little tummies to the cold. T-shirts can however be worn over bodysuits as an extra, often more interesting layer, when the weather allows. Look for stretchy necks or ones that open wide with buttons or poppers.

Coats – new babies who are lying flat in their pram or buggy can be kept warm with blankets, wraps and footmuffs or raincovers so don't really need coats. A comfy little quilted coat can however be useful if you'll use a sling/carrier a lot (be careful not to overdress your baby in this scenario as your body warmth will also help keep them cosy).

Only once your baby is older and sitting up in a buggy will they really need a winter coat. Look for breathable fabrics. Something thinner will work in spring and autumn too and can be layered with cardigans to add warmth.

For older babies in winter, buy one or two relatively lightweight, breathable coats that allow room for layers underneath.

Shoes – baby booties and shoes are unnecessary before babies can walk properly and have an annoying tendency to fall off and get lost. That said, they look cute – if you're tempted, choose very soft ones which won't constrict your baby's foot growth.

Bibs – newborn bibs are a godsend if your baby is the sicky type but you'll probably receive some as gifts, so don't buy too many in advance. Choose either the stretchy popover type that go over the baby's head or those with a side fastening press stud – much easier than those that fasten at the back of the neck. Avoid tie-bibs completely and steer clear of Velcro fastenings unless you can trust yourself to always do the Velcro up before they go in the wash – otherwise that gorgeous designer outfit that we advised you not to buy will come out of the washing machine stuck to the bib Velcro.

Twin tip: don't be tempted to stint on clothing. Given you'll have twice the babies and consequently half the time for laundry, you *will* definitely need double the amount for a single baby.

> **Parent panel tip:** "I do a big shop for clothes for the children in the sales – I work out what size they'll be in the corresponding season next year and pick up some real bargains and designer stuff I couldn't otherwise afford."

3

Changing nappies

Shopping list

- ✓ Nappies
- ✓ Cotton wool pads and/or wipes
- ✓ Nappy rash cream
- ✓ Lidded nappy bin and two laundry nets (if using washables)
- ✓ Changing bag or equivalent
- ✓ Muslin cloths or towelling squares
- ✓ Nappy sacks
- ? Nappy disposal unit
- ? Changing mat
- ✗ Wipes warmer

For changing units see page 97.

NAPPIES

Clearly nappies will play a major part in your life for the next few years with much buying, changing and disposing/washing of them. Nappies and their contents will invade your shopping list, your thoughts and even your conversations. We guarantee you'll have a few chats about the contents of your baby's nappy or the staggering number of bowel movements they've produced in a given day.

You might not want to hear this (we're going to tell you anyway) but each baby produces around 100kg of poo and 250 litres of wee in their first two-and-a-half years – thankfully not all at once. In fact, you'll be changing 5,000 or so nappies between your baby's birth and the time they graduate to the potty or loo.

The great washables versus disposables debate

Even if you've never changed a nappy in your life, it'd be hard to have missed the arguments over whether disposables or washable/cloth nappies are the more environmentally friendly.

In the washables camp, you'll hear that disposables create huge amounts of landfill waste that take decades to biodegrade and produce methane gas, contributing to global warming. Cloth sceptics counter that laundering washables consumes copious water and energy, turning this supposedly eco-friendly option a rather paler shade of green.

Studies exist which support both views but many have been commissioned by interested parties with their own agendas. The UK's Environment Agency undertook perhaps the most comprehensive research, trying to get to the bottom (excuse the pun) of this tricky nappy debate. Their conclusion was that overall there's little difference between the environmental cost of the two types. Fans of 'cloth' claim this study was flawed as it assumed nappies weren't washed in the most eco-friendly manner. So for now it remains hard to know what the truth is and which way is best. And to complicate things further, you also need to consider …

… the middle ground (with less landfill in it)

Your choice isn't confined to creating huge amounts of landfill or gigantic loads of laundry, there's also a middle ground in the form of 'eco-disposables'. These offer the convenience of disposables but are at least partly bio-degradable and have been manufactured with an eye on environmental issues, for example, avoiding the use of chlorine and chemical gels. Of course, as a throwaway product, they use up resources in production and transportation and the methane problem remains, but they are more eco-friendly than standard disposables.

Unfortunately, eco-disposables aren't that widely available. The Nature brand can be found in some supermarkets plus Boots and Mothercare, but others such as Moltex, Tushies Gel and Bambo are mainly sold online or in specialist 'greener' nursery shops and some health food stores. Add to this that most eco-disposables are more expensive and some don't perform as well as the likes of Pampers and this could explain why their use isn't more commonplace.

Of the brands we've tested, we like Bambo and Seventh Generation best – they're soft, absorbent and slim-fitting. Bambos cost around 1p to 2p more than Pampers per nappy which adds up to an extra £50 to £100 over one baby's nappy-wearing years. Nature are cheaper, being comparably priced to Pampers and Huggies but feel inflexible and bulky.

It's worth getting trial packs of several brands to see which you like best.

Verdict: despite question marks over how bio-degradable eco-disposables really are, these are a good compromise for those whose conscience is troubled by standard disposables.

★ *Bambo, Seventh Generation.*

More about washables

Washable nappies have come a tremendously long way since the days of terry squares that needed folding and fastening with scary-looking pins. These are still available and are the cheapest nappy option but modern alternatives are more absorbent and considerably easier to use, especially if you add a flushable liner to catch 'solids', making the cleaning process less grim.

Yes, washables cost more to buy initially but they're still cheaper than disposables in the long run and some local authorities offer free trial packs or subsidies to help get you started with washables. You can also use them for more than one child or sell them once they're no longer needed (believe it or not there's strong demand for second-hand nappies).

The challenge brought by the revolution in cloth nappies is choosing between the many different 'systems'. We can only cover the basics here but there are some excellent cloth nappy specialists online who can advise further – try **www.thenappylady.com**.

A word of warning: don't cough up for a full set of washables before testing them out. Get trial packs and see if cloth is really for you and which brand you like – they vary a lot in absorbency, ease of use and fit (some are better for chubby babies, others for slimmer ones).

The main buying decisions:

1. Which style of cloth nappy to go for?

Broadly speaking there are four types of washable nappy.

Cloth nappy types:

Flat/pre-fold

DESCRIPTION: Traditional terry or muslin squares that are either flat or have a thicker panel stitched in (pre-folds). Flats are fastened with pins or 'nappi nippas' and both types need covering with a wrap. Pre-folds are the most commonly used by nappy laundering services.

PROS:

- Cheap
- Widely available
- Less bulky and can be folded to fit all shapes of baby
- Quick drying
- Flats are one-size so no need to upgrade to bigger ones later.

CONS:

- Fiddly to use
- Can be troublesome for any babysitters who aren't used to them.

EXPENSE: **£**

Shaped

DESCRIPTION: Shaped like disposables. They also go under a wrap. Either one-size or sized (see page 26).

PROS:

- Easy to wash
- No folding required.

CONS:

- Can be bulky (especially one-size versions)
- Easier to use than flats but fiddlier than all-in-ones.

EXPENSE: **££**

Pocket

DESCRIPTION: These are shaped with a waterproof outer layer and softer inner layer with a pocket to which you add absorbent material. No additional wrap is needed.

PROS:

- Can control absorbency by using different 'stuffing' in the pocket

- Fast drying as come apart
- No folding required
- Relatively slim fitting

CONS:

- Fiddlier than all-in-ones as they require 'stuffing'
- Possibly more prone to leaks

EXPENSE: **££**

All-in-one

DESCRIPTION: A waterproof outer layer with an integral absorbent inner, shaped like a disposable nappy

PROS:

- Easy to use (so especially good for daycare, babysitters etc.)

CONS:

- Take longer to dry as thicker
- Wear out quicker as the whole thing needs washing after each wear (separate wraps don't usually)

EXPENSE: **£££**

Verdict: we prefer shaped nappies as they're easier to use than flats and pre-folds. Generally we also favour two-pieces over all-in-ones as they usually have better absorbency, are quicker to dry and more economical. Having a few all-in-ones can be useful for when you're out or for other carers such as babysitters who will probably find them simpler to use.

2. Which fabrics?

Wraps and outer layers are typically made from polyester fleece, coated cotton or wool. Inner layers are usually made from cotton, fleece, bamboo or hemp cloth. Which you go for is a matter of personal preference but inners should be soft but absorbent, and outers/wraps waterproof but quick drying.

3. Sized or one-size nappies?

Some washable nappies are sized, others are adjustable and designed to fit from birth to when potty training occurs. With sized nappies, you have to buy new ones once or twice as your baby grows.

'One-size-fits-all' nappies generally work out cheaper but sized versions tend to fit better throughout, especially if your baby is particularly slim, chubby or a late potty trainer, but they are more expensive.

Verdict: invest in sized nappies if you can afford them. They fit newborns better and are less likely to leak. They're a sensible buy if you plan more than one child as wear and tear will be less than with a one-size nappy. Later switchers from disposables to cloth should find 'birth-to-potty' one sizers fine though.

Tots Bots Bamboozles (sized, shaped two-pieces), Onelife (one-size, shaped two-piece nappies), Pop-in Nappy System (see below), Kooshies (sized all-in-ones), Motherease (one-size, shaped two-pieces), Bambino Mio (sized, pre-fold two pieces).

Product showcase – we've been impressed by the new Pop-in Nappy System. Its clever design solves some of the problems of other cloth nappies. It comprises three separate pieces which easily popper together to effectively form an all-in-one. These separate parts mean it's quicker to dry than standard all-in-ones but it's easier to get on a baby than a two-piece. One size should fit all the way through the nappy years as it's highly-adjustable too, making it good value for money.

Pop-in nappies

How many?

This partly depends on how often you're willing to put your washing machine on. Assuming you wash on alternate days and line or air dry rather than tumble dry, you should buy 18 to 20 nappies, be they nappy inserts for two-pieces or all-in-ones. For two-piece nappy systems, four wraps should suffice as they needn't be washed after every nappy change.

Look for:

- *Fit and sizing that works for your baby* – some brands are better for slimmer babies and others for chubbier ones. There's an element of trial and error with this.
- *Absorbency* – leaky nappies can wake babies up at night so choose fabric that's particularly absorbent or brands where you can add a booster pad if needed for night-time.
- *Drying time and method* – some wraps can't be tumble-dried, so check if that's your preferred drying method (it isn't very eco-friendly though). Some materials dry quicker than others – fleece is a good, fast-drying choice. All-in-ones take longer to dry so you might need to buy more.
- *Breathable wraps/outers* – help avoid nappy rash and keep your baby cool in hot weather. PUL (which stands for something very long, dull and technical-sounding) is better than plastic or PVC coatings for breathability.
- *Fastening method* – Velcro is faster to do up than poppers but tends to get caught on other items in the laundry. A few nappies tie on but these are annoying to do up and best avoided.

- The *cost from birth to potty training* – try and focus on this rather than the initial outlay.

Nappy liners and boosters

Adding a liner to washable nappies helps keep a baby's skin drier and makes it easier to dispose of poo. They can be washable or disposable but biodegradable. The better disposable ones can be flushed down the loo after use.

You can also buy booster pads (typically fleece or towelling) to add extra absorbency for night-time, or alternatively use a folded muslin or towelling square. Some nappy systems offer booster pads as part of the package.

> **Parent panel tip:** "We used disposables for the first few hectic weeks but switched to reusables once everything calmed down a bit. If we're away we still use disposables, although we try and stick to the greener brands."

Washing cloth nappies. Some local councils and companies run nappy laundering services. Their eco-credentials are debatable, as although 'commercial' washing methods are greener, the collection and delivery mileage clocked up also has to be taken into consideration. A laundering service will provide you with freshly-washed pre-fold nappies each week and take away used ones. You still need to purchase and wash the wraps yourself. If you launder at home, and the majority of cloth users do, ideally skip the tumble drier. Using an eco-friendly laundry liquid/powder or a detergent alternative such as Eco Balls can also help keep things greener.

TIP: Cloth nappies are bulkier than disposables so you might need to buy one size larger clothing to accommodate the nappy.

STANDARD DISPOSABLES

Disposable nappies are undeniably convenient and are used by the vast majority of parents. Most contain a material called polyacrylates, which when wet becomes a gel, absorbing many times its own weight in liquid. Some also have a stay-dry layer rather like on sanitary towels.

The best-known brands are Pampers and Huggies, although supermarket and other 'own label' brands can be cheaper and often perform just as well. The absorbency, bulkiness, fit and softness of nappy brands does vary, so try different ones and see which you prefer and which fit your baby best.

Look for:

- *Cost per nappy* – different brands sell different-sized packs, making price comparisons tricky – some supermarkets display a price per nappy which is more useful (newborn nappies tend to cost from 11p to 16p each). There will almost always be one brand on offer in supermarkets, so you could swap and change if money is tight or stock up when your favoured brand is discounted (don't go too far with this as your baby will need different sizes and possibly styles as they grow). Bigger packs save money – the same nappies in larger 'economy' packs cost around 25% less per nappy than those in small packs.
- *A good fit* – as with cloth nappies some will suit your baby's shape better than others. Larger gaps around the thighs and top could mean leaks.
- *Lack of bulkiness* – especially once a baby starts getting mobile, a bulky nappy can annoy them and hamper movement.

- *Softness* – some brands are a bit scratchy around the edges and this can irritate sensitive skin.
- *The right 'stage' nappy for your baby* – newborn nappies are designed to absorb and hold in the runnier poo new babies produce, whereas nappies for older babies offer greater flexibility and stretchiness for crawlers and walkers.
- *Size* – look at the weight range and move to the next size when your baby reaches the relevant minimum weight – the bigger size will offer more absorbency.

How many?

Newborns can get through 12 nappies a day, although more typically eight. Older babies might only need four to six changes daily.

Pampers (for newborns), Pampers or Tesco (for older babies).

So, which way to go?

Until this reusables or disposables debate is put to bed (which at this rate could take as long as the biodegradation of a disposable nappy), it's down to you to decide which route works best for your new family. Issues to consider include convenience, eco-friendliness, comfort, absorbency and cost.

Unless you're insistent on using cloth all the time, it will be more convenient to start with eco- or standard disposables for at least the first few days post-birth, before switching over.

NAPPY TYPES – A COMPARISON

	Washables	Standard disposables	Eco-disposables
Convenience for parents	Low (storage and laundering needed)	High	High
Landfill contribution	None	High	Lower if biodegradable
Energy and resources used in production	Low (15 to 20 nappies are produced once and can be re-used for another baby)	High (around 5,000 nappies for each child)	Moderate to high (eco-nappy manufacturing tends to be greener)
Energy and resources used in laundering	Medium to high depending on temperature and drying method	None	None
Comfort for babies	Usually high (soft cotton)	Variable	Variable – some brands are a bit scratchy and stiff
Absorbency and 'leak proofness'	Medium	High	Medium to high
Initial cost	High	Low	Low
Ongoing cost	Low – laundering costs only	High	High
Total cost (estimate assuming 5,000 nappy changes)	£400	£550-600	£600-800

Other pros and cons

WASHABLES

- Soft on sensitive skin
- Can be inconvenient when travelling
- Need to take dirty nappies home when out, rather than throwing them away
- Bulky – clothes can be too tight in nappy area

- Babies in washables tend to potty train more easily as they understand 'being wet'.

STANDARD DISPOSABLES

- Your outside bin quickly fills up (problematic for those with fortnightly refuse collections or more than one child in nappies).

ECO DISPOSABLES

- Not as widely sold as standard disposables
- Some are bulkier than standard disposables.
- Refuse considerations are the same as for regular disposables.

CHANGING ACCESSORIES

Nappy disposal

You have two options here – a fancy unit that wraps the nappy and its enclosed 'delights', storing them in a relatively odour-proof (and inquisitive toddler-proof) unit that only needs emptying when full, or a bog-standard lidded nappy pail, possibly with scented nappy sacks to mask smells. Basic nappy pails are cheaper but need emptying more frequently to prevent the pong getting too bad.

We find the units that require cartridges a bit of a swizz – the bins themselves are sold relatively cheaply, sucking you into shelling out for cartridges for a couple of years. Those that wrap nappies using normal bin bags are more expensive initially and bulkier but cost less overall and are more convenient.

Verdict: a standard cheap nappy pail plus sacks works fine if you don't mind more frequent bin emptying. If you want a disposal system, we favour those using standard bin bags to the ones with cartridges as they're cheaper.

Disposal units: Boots Nappysafe, or Vital (both use bin bags rather than refill cartridges), Korbel Bin (uses refills made from biodegradable plastic).

Nappy sacks: Tesco (good size, scented nappy bags)
Degradable nappy sacks: Naturebotts, Earth Friendly Baby

TIP: If you do go for a cartridge based nappy unit, reduce spending on refills by confining use to pooey nappies and putting 'wee-only' ones (they don't smell) in your regular bin.

Nappy storage

Used cloth nappies are probably best stored in a mesh nappy bag within a lidded nappy pail. On wash day, you can lift the bag straight out and into the washing machine, with no need to handle anything unpleasant. You can store nappies 'dry' or add nappy soak or tea tree oil to the bucket. Buy a second mesh bag for when the other one is in the wash.

A waterproof zipped sack (often called a 'wet bag') can be used for carrying dirty nappies home when you're out.

Wipes

Wipes come in unscented, scented, biodegradable and 'natural' varieties. Most midwives recommend starting with cotton wool (pads are better than balls) and water instead of wipes, as it will be gentler for newborn skin. Beyond the early days, wipes are more convenient, especially when out, and most parents find those that are for sensitive skin or contain only natural ingredients tend to be fine even for delicate newborn skin. Fragrance is certainly best-avoided – and indeed unnecessary.

Wipes vary in price but there will almost always be one brand on offer in any given store – so if you have a favourite brand, stock up when it's discounted.

Those of a green and/or money-saving mindset can avoid disposable wipes or cut down on their use by buying or making reusable ones – fleece or terry are effective for nappy changing wipes and muslin cloths work well for meal times with older babies and toddlers.

When going out, decant wipes into a small wipes holder (included with some changing bags) or a re-sealable freezer bag. This saves carrying a full heavy pack of wipes around or paying more for the slimline travel packs.

TIP: Wipes dry out easily and the supposedly stay shut sticky lids don't tend to. Store the packet upside down to prevent drying or look out for free storage tubs with jumbo packs.

E45 or Simple. Natural options: Earth Friendly Baby, Natracare and Nature.

Nappy cream

Barrier nappy creams prevent nappy rash in the first place, whereas treatment creams clear it up. Barrier creams are best avoided with disposables as they reduce absorbency.

Metanium,Sudocrem, Earth Friendly Baby, Neal's Yard.

Wipes warmers

Despite their popularity in the US, these are baulked at by many British parents. Yes, some babies hate cold wipes but most will at least tolerate them, especially if they don't know any different as you've never warmed them. Generally warmers are a faff and extra expense you can do without. Only worth considering if your baby consistently squeals at cold wipes.

Standard changing mats

You can use a large towel under your baby but changing mats are inexpensive and make for a comfortable, easy to clean surface for nappy changes. Some are plain and functional, others have decidedly funky coverings.

Most come with slightly raised sides but these have limited use when it comes to the somewhat impossible challenge of keeping mobile older babies in place at change time. Waterproof vinyl is more practical than towelling – you can line it with a muslin or towel to make it less of a cold shock for your baby's bum.

Look for: *a wipe-able, washable surface.*

ZPM Multimats, Mamas & Papas ones with little pillows, Whole New World Mats.

TIP: Once your baby gets mobile, use distraction to encourage co-operation at changing time. Keep an interesting toy only for changing time or invest in a wall-mounted mobile (Infantino make a good one).

Disposable changing mats

These are extremely useful when out and about. Whilst not terribly eco-friendly they're not as bad as they sound, as they can be reused many times. A pack of 12 lasted us about 18 months. Their great benefit is, if they do get soiled or used on some really grubby changing unit when you're out (and believe us some of these are revolting), you can just chuck them away, rather than carting a skanky mat home with you to clean it up. They're lighter and more compact than most travel/roll-up changing mats (although rather less padded) and can double as protection when potty training.

★ *Pampers ChangeMats.*

Changing bags

Another 'not strictly essential but very useful' buy, these are purpose-designed for dragging around the endless amounts of gubbins you'll need to take with you whenever you go out with your baby. Most have pockets for bottles, soiled clothes and so on.

They used to be dull, functional affairs and indeed there are still some boring ones on the market, but look harder and there are gorgeous, covetable versions too that wouldn't be out of place on a catwalk (and not all with designer price tags). There are plenty of different styles – rucksacks, messenger bags (popular with dads), ones that fit over pram handles, extra large ones for twins – choose whichever you prefer.

Some include a changing mat and bottle insulator/holder but if the one you want doesn't, these can be added separately. As important as practicalities is a style and a design you like, because you could be carrying this one bag around for the next two years.

Look for:

- A *wipe-able interior and exterior*
- *Several pockets* to separate feeding and nappy changing stuff, keep bottles or food jars upright and help you find things easily (although conversely too many pockets defeats the purpose)
- A *design that others using the bag can live with* (if both mum and dad will carry the bag, girly floral might be unwise)
- *Decent capacity* – like it or not, you'll need something big. There's a lot to go in there – spare clothes, bottles, snacks, nappies, wipes, toys, kitchen sinks … we could go on

Do you really need one?

You will need some sort of large practical bag for your baby's gear. Some parents use a regular bag instead of a purpose-designed number and add a compact changing pouch (see page 38).

Verdict: styles and designs are a personal thing but remember there's no need to settle for dull (unless that's what you want). Go beyond the high street to find more original designs (**Happybags.co.uk** and **Changingbags.co.uk** have an unusually wide selection).

OiOi, Skip-hop, Pink Lining, Stork Sak, Baby Mel.

What to put in your changing bag

- Nappies
- Wipes
- Nappy cream
- Nappy sacks/wet bag for washables
- Portable changing mat
- Muslins
- Bibs
- Spare clothes for your baby (vest and sleepsuit)
- Dummies (if using them)
- Bottle and formula dispenser (unless breastfeeding)
- A favourite toy/teether
- Hand sanitising gel
- Spare top for you if your baby is the sicky type

Portable changing pouches

If you don't want a dedicated changing bag, you can buy handy little pouches to use in any bag. They open out into a mat, hold two or three nappies and have a compartment to hold wipes.

First Years Fold and Go, Oi Oi Compact Mat, Skip Hop Pronto.

Muslins and towelling squares

Boring they might be but these are nonetheless fab. They're essential for mopping up all those baby secretions and much more eco-friendly than wipes.

We recommend getting six towelling squares and twelve muslins. This sounds a lot but they're cheap and have loads of uses – lining changing mats, makeshift bibs, mopping up spillages. You'll probably also have one semi-permanently draped over your shoulder in the early days to protect your clothes from baby puke.

Some shops sell coloured and patterned ones – useful if you want to identify your baby's vomit-covered cloth rather than someone else's at a post-natal group. Organic versions are also available.

Posh, patterned 'burp cloths' are a stylish alternative for special occasions such as weddings when a muslin draped over a shoulder could spoil your look! Try Spongy Feet, Dwell Baby burp cloths, Living Textiles or Zorbit for coloured muslin squares.

4

Bathing

Shopping list

✓ Soft towel solely for your baby's use

✓ Baby nail clippers or scissors

✓ Flannel or sponge

? Baby bath

? Newborn bath support

? Bath ring (for use from around six months)

? Bath thermometer

? Toiletries

✗ Travel baby baths (unless you'll stay somewhere without a normal bath)

✗ Bath dressers

✗ Baby bath stands

✗ Bath 'sets' (such as a baby bath plus towel, top and tail bowl, toiletries)

✗ Top and tail bowls

Bathing a newborn the first few times can be daunting, with you juggling a slippery and possibly screaming baby, washing their nooks and crannies, calming them and grabbing sponges and a towel. At moments like this you wonder why God/evolution (according to your viewpoint) didn't give us more hands.

But never fear, the baby products industry *did* invent baby bath supports and a few other useful products which make this whole 'ordeal' more manageable.

Can't you just use the kitchen sink?

Yes, you can bathe babies in the kitchen sink but if you're anything like us, especially when we had newborns, your sink will be way too full of dirty dishes to fit a Barbie doll in, never mind a baby. If you are more domesticated than us (and that's not difficult), a large kitchen sink makes a good first bath and can be easier on your back as there's no bending over the bath's side to reach the baby. But it will require you to drag all your bath-time stuff downstairs and we find most people prefer to stick to the bathroom these days anyway.

BATH SUPPORTS

Regardless of whether you use a full-size or baby bath, these reduce the stress of bath-time considerably, by freeing up your hands. You can manage without (but it is trickier), or get in the bath with your baby, but supports are cheap to buy and can easily be bought second-hand or borrowed.

> **Parent panel tip:** "When Isabella was on the bath support I worried she'd get cold as the water wasn't covering her, so we'd put a wet flannel over her and pour warm water onto it to keep her warmer."

Types of bath support

1 *Foam/ sponge* – a soft wedge-shaped support, usually with a baby-shaped indentation. Probably the comfiest option for the baby but

they tend to go mildewy (the support not the baby). You'll have to remember to wring it out, and even then they can still get a bit whiffy (both the baby and the support). You'll probably have to keep a hand on the baby using these which, in our view, rather defeats the purpose.

2 *Fabric* – these range from a simple frame with towelling stretched across it to fancy bath 'chairs' with little head pillows. Comfortable and practical but avoid anything that isn't mildew resistant unless the cover is machine washable. As above, you might need to keep a hand hovering by your baby to stop them slipping off.

3 *Moulded plastic* – although these are hard plastic, they are contoured so they 'fit' the baby's shape and are definitely the most practical and easy to clean. Due to the high praise they receive from parents, it would seem that babies are comfy enough in them and we definitely favour these of the three types.

Look for:

- *Something that won't go mildewy* – fabric or foam supports can quickly become mildewy. Having to remember to wring out the support after every bath, when dealing with getting the baby dry and dressed is a pain and doesn't always prevent this for long anyway. If you do prefer a fabric support, ensure the cover is washable but remember this will be another item to add to your huge washing pile.

- *A support that really will be hands-free* – note that we aren't suggesting you don't keep a very close eye on your baby – you must never ever leave a baby unattended in the bath.

★ *Tigex moulded bath supports.*

Twin tip: Get two moulded plastic supports. Since they don't require you to keep a hand on the babies in them, they're the only feasible way for one person to bathe two babies at once.

BABY BATHS

Do you need a baby bath as well as a support?

Not really, as you can just place the support in the main bath. The advantage of using the support within a baby bath is that it will save water but the baby bath will be an extra bit of kit to store in your bathroom.

If you do want a baby bath, like bath supports, they're well-suited to being bought second-hand or borrowed. There are three types of baby bath – standard, rest-on-rim and bucket baths:

Types of baby bath

1 *'Standard'*– cheap (around £10) and sometimes cheerfully decorated with cute/hideous (depending on your taste) character motifs. They'll last until your baby is around six months, and can be used with or without a support (without, means holding your baby with one hand) but if you're using a support you can skip these.

Look for: sturdy plastic, a non-slip base (if you won't use a support) and easy-to-grip handles or sides if you'll move the bath between rooms when it's full of water.

+ Cheap
+ Use less water and quicker to fill than a full-sized bath
− Take up extra storage space
− Require a bath support too for hands-free bathing.

2 *'Rest-on-rim'* – rest over the sides of the main bath. Because they're higher up, you needn't bend over so much to reach the baby – a relief if you have a bad back. Our favourite is made by Tigex and has detachable rests so it can also be used inside the adult bath or on the floor like a standard baby bath. It fits most baths but do check before buying. Again, these baths require a support too if you want to solve the 'not having enough hands' problem. Worth paying the extra £10 or so if you want a baby bath.

- ⊕ Easier on your back
- ⊖ More expensive than standard baby baths
- ⊖ Not all models fit all baths
- ⊖ Require a bath support too for hands-free bathing

★ *Tigex Bath with Adjustable Arms, Mothercare Supabath.*

3 *Bucket baths ('Tummytub' and similar)* – essentially a transparent plastic bucket, allowing the baby to sit snugly in a familiar foetal position during bathing. Many mums and midwives are fans. Note that you will need to support a newborn's head when they're in the tub so although they're more supportive than standard baby baths, these don't allow you to be totally hands free.

- ⊕ Comforting and soothing for babies as sitting in a foetal position surrounded by warm water is a throw-back to being in the womb
- ⊕ They're compact and good when travelling
- ⊕ Much easier to move between rooms when filled than regular baby baths
- ⊕ Use up less water
- ⊖ More expensive
- ⊖ Getting the baby in and out can be awkward at first
- ⊖ You'll need to keep a hand on a young baby

- No room for older babies to play and splash about although babies used to these won't know what they're missing and tend to want to stay in them as long as possible.

These will probably either appeal to you or not. If you do get one, it might take a couple of goes to get used to but it will be worth persevering. Although they're recommended for up to eight months, we know of older babies who still like going in theirs.

Tummytub.

Verdict: go for a rest-on-rim bath if you have back problems. If not use either the big bath with a moulded plastic support or a bucket bath, depending on what appeals to you.

OTHER BATH-TIME ITEMS

Bath rings

These plastic rings support older babies, allowing them to sit up in the bath without toppling over. They're suitable from around six months (when a newborn bath support will have been outgrown), but the window of time from then until your baby is able to sit unsupported on a non-slip bathmat will probably be short so these aren't useful for long. Many parents also find them awkward to lift their baby in and out of.

Verdict: not worth buying – borrow one or manage without.

Travel baby baths (inflatable and folding baths)

If there's a normal bath at your destination it's cheaper and easier to cope for a few days with that. If you'll stay somewhere without a normal bath, the inflatable ones take up less space and weigh less than the folding variety.

Bath dressers

Unless you have a serious back problem and can't bend over even to use a rest-on-rim bath, please, please avoid wasting money on these. They're expensive, ugly, take up loads of space and their useful life is short. They also involve carrying a heavy bath full of water to the dresser or the tiresome task of filling it with jugs of water – either way there's a good chance you'll slosh water everywhere on the way. If you do feel the need to buy one, those with a pipe can at least be emptied directly into your sink or bath (it won't help with the filling).

Bath stands

Designed to save you from kneeling bath-side but the effort involved in lifting a heavy bath full of water on and off is almost as challenging to your back muscles.

Bathing 'sets'

Some retailers sell bundles of bathing items including perhaps a baby bath, bath thermometer, towel and top and tail bowl, sometimes decorated with a theme. These probably won't save you money unless you want or need all the items and they rarely contain the best products of each type anyway.

Baby towels

Special baby towels with hoods look cute but any soft towel solely for your baby's use will do. All too many baby towels (sometimes called 'cuddle robes') are made of disappointingly thin terry towelling so lack absorbency and cosiness and tend to be so small that your baby will need a bigger towel within a few months.

Verdict: manage without and use a normal soft towel (baby towels are a popular gift so you might receive one or two anyway).

> **Product showcase** – the apron-style baby towels from Cuddledry are the exception to our view that hooded baby towels aren't worth buying. They fasten around your neck leaving your hands free to lift your baby out of the bath, thereby avoiding that tricky moment when you must hold the towel and simultaneously grab the baby (hoping that if you drop anything it's the towel). They're quite expensive (around £25 each) but make a real difference if you often do bath time alone and are wonderfully thick, soft organic towelling. They're also generously-sized so will last through to toddlerhood. One should suffice as you can manage with a normal towel when the Cuddledry one is being washed.
>
> *Cuddledry towels*

Bath thermometers

The time-honoured trick of dunking your elbow in the bath to check the water temperature means these aren't necessary. If you do feel the need to get one, we recommend those that double as room thermometers as you'll get more use out of them.

Philips, Beaba.

Top and tail bowls

These are plastic bowls, split into two sections to separate the water for 'topping and tailing' (wiping the baby's face and bottom in the early weeks when daily baths aren't necessary). They're cheap (£3 to £5) but entirely pointless when any two ordinary clean bowls will do, plus you'll probably only top and tail for a short period before more frequent baths and baby wipes take over.

Verdict: a complete waste of cash.

Toiletries

Rewind a few decades and new mums brandished bottles of baby bath, baby lotion and talc aplenty. Nowadays there's more of a 'back-to-basics' approach since many parents worry about using chemical ingredients. In fact, most midwives advise that plain water is perfectly adequate for newborn bathing – no potions are required – and that olive oil is one of the best, most natural ways to moisturise baby skin.

Meanwhile, talcum powder has been thrown out with the baby's bath-water – studies have shown even small amounts can be harmful if inhaled and besides, with modern nappies and decent nappy cream it isn't needed.

When it comes to shampoos, newborn hair rarely needs washing and even that of older babies only needs it infrequently. This is a very good thing because most little people aren't exactly ecstatic about having it done and many scream through the process. Some shampoos seem to sting eyes more than others but when it comes to that 'no more tears' claim of a well-known brand, well, there isn't a shampoo around that can solve the problem of babies hating their faces being drenched with water.

TIP: If your baby gets upset by hair washing, the visors and flexible jugs that stop water going on the face can help prevent tears at bath-time.

If and when you want to introduce lotions and potions for your baby, there are plenty of organic and natural ranges, although they tend to cost a bit more than the likes of Johnson's. A look at the lengthy lists of chemical ingredients on the back of most standard baby toiletry bottles can be a convincing argument that it's worth paying the extra to go organic .

Burt's Bees, Green People, Halos N Horns, Beginning by Maclaren, Earth Friendly Baby, Green Baby.

GROOMING GEAR

Nail clippers and scissors

Tiny nails grow remarkably quickly and are challenging to cut when Junior is wriggling about (our best baby manicure tip is to do it when they're asleep). Some people find little nail clippers easier, others favour round-ended baby nail scissors – there's no right answer so choose whichever you prefer. A few parents bite or tear their baby's finger nails when they're newborn and their nails are soft. Whichever method you go with, a small nail file can be useful to smooth off jagged edges.

Hairbrushes

New babies are usually somewhat lacking in the hair department, so you might well assume they don't need hairbrushes. However, they can still be useful, as arguably brushing the scalp with circular strokes daily helps prevent cradle cap (scaly patches that appear on some young babies' scalps) and stimulates hair growth. Regardless, the brush won't be wasted as sooner or later junior will sprout more hair.

Strong bristled brushes are more effective than the very soft ones.

Kent baby hairbrushes.

5

Feeding

Shopping list

✓ Two feeding bottles (six if you plan to mainly bottle-feed)

✓ Three breastfeeding bras

✓ Breast pads

✓ Nipple cream

✓ Steriliser

✓ Highchair

✓ Weaning spoons and bowls

✓ Training cups

? Breast pump (*essential if you develop mastitis or engorgement)

? Breastmilk storage containers/bags

? Formula milk (essential if bottle-feeding from birth)

? Formula dispenser

? Breastfeeding pillow

? Nipple shields

? Baby food blender

✗ Breastfeeding clothes

✗ Bottlewarmer

BREASTFEEDING ACCESSORIES

There's been a major push in recent years to encourage mums to breastfeed, with a Government recommendation that breastfeeding until at least six months is best. We're not going to debate the merits of breast versus formula milk here as there's plenty of information elsewhere on this. Some mums find breastfeeding a doddle, others struggle (attending breastfeeding classes, reading up and seeking advice can make all the difference) and although you can manage with just the 'equipment' nature provides (!), there are a few products that can ease things along.

Breast pumps

These allow mums to express milk which can then be given to the baby in a bottle. It is possible to express by hand without a pump but most women prefer to use one.

We must warn you that although worthy, expressing can make you feel like a cow in a milking parlour. Your boobs being squeezed by a machine until milk squirts out certainly isn't one of the most glamorous aspects of parenthood.

Do you really need one?

If you're going to solely formula-feed, then no.

Otherwise, you will need one if any of the following apply:

- you're returning to work and want your baby to have breast milk when you're not with them.
- you'd like someone else to give your baby a bottle of breast milk occasionally so you can have a break.
- your baby is hospitalised, has a feeding problem or is too ill to feed

directly from the breast but you want them to have breast milk (although note that pumps are nearly always available in special care baby units and some hospitals lend them out for home use in such scenarios).

- your breasts become engorged (too full of milk) or you start developing mastitis (inflammation of the breast) – a pump will help ease these conditions.

When do you need it?

We recommend buying a pump before the birth but leaving it unopened and keeping the receipt in case you don't need it or find you'd prefer a different type.

Hiring a pump

You can rent 'hospital grade' breast pumps [try the National Childbirth Trust or **www.expressyourselfmums.com**] but unless you'll only need it for a very short period, this usually works out more expensive than buying. The better 'consumer' models for sale these days are more than adequate.

TIP: if you're returning to work, start expressing well in advance to get your baby used to a bottle – some babies take a while to adapt if they've only ever been breastfed.

The main buying decisions:

1 Manual or electric?

Electric pumps cost more but are usually quicker and less tiring for your hands. If you'll express every day, then they're a must. Indeed if you're likely to express even a moderate amount we still think it's worth paying extra for an electric pump. The only exception is if you have an exceptionally good milk supply or will only express very occasionally, in which case you could make do with a manual (you will only know this post-birth so if the pump you originally bought is no longer right for you, exchange it).

Medela Swing (very efficient single electric), Medela Mini Electric (noisy but cheaper and adequate for less frequent expressing).

2 Double or single?

Double pumps allow simultaneous expressing from both breasts, speeding the process up. Singles are generally cheaper and will suffice for most mums, but if you're going to be expressing on a very regular basis, a double is worth investing in.

Ameda Egnell Lactaline, Medela Pump in Style (both pricey but powerful and very portable. The Medela fastens into its own backpack, excellent for expressing at work.)

Don't pay extra for:

Integrated pump plus feeding 'systems' – some manufacturers boast that their pumps 'integrate' with their baby bottles for convenience. However, that particular manufacturer's bottles might not suit your baby (breastfed babies can be very fussy when first bottle-feeding and the teat brand can make a significant difference) and besides, expressing into any sterile container and pouring the milk into any baby bottle isn't so much extra hassle.

Breast milk storage

Expressed milk can be stored in sterile containers or bags in the fridge or freezer. Some pumps integrate with specific manufacturers' storage bags/bottles but generally you can use any sterile canister or any make of milk storage bag. If you use bags, sit them in a sterile container to prevent wasting milk in case of leaks.

Medela Pump and Save Bags, Lansinoh, Avent or Boots Breastmilk Bags, Medela Breastmilk Storage Pots.

Breast pads

Breast pads sit in your bra, soaking up the milk leaks which are pretty inevitable post-birth (and sometimes in pregnancy) and which can cause soggy patches on clothing. There are disposable and reusable versions. Disposables are more convenient but less eco-friendly (although you can now buy biodegradable ones). Reusables (either washable fabric or silicone pads) are the more cost-effective and greener choice.

Lansinoh's washable or disposable pads, Johnson's disposables, Natracare bio-degradable pads.

Shields and protectors

These small plastic shields sit between your nipples and the baby's mouth during feeds. They're not normally necessary unless you have inverted nipples, a baby who is too weak to feed without them or has tongue tie/a palate problem, or you have extremely sore nipples and have tried other remedies.

According to lactation experts the problem with shields is that they can inhibit breastfeeding if babies get too used to the feel of them and they can start to refuse feeds without. Although for this reason they are best avoided if possible, in the situations mentioned above they can be beneficial. Generally, if you have inverted or flat nipples it's worthwhile purchasing a set in advance, otherwise just be aware of where you can get them if needed at short notice.

Breast shells are less problematic as they aren't worn during feeds. They are also silicon covers but go in your bra to prevent sore nipples chafing against clothing. Some collect excess milk so it can be poured into a container for use. If you won't use this milk, add cotton wool to the shells to prevent a mess when you remove them.

Verdict: most women manage without shields and protectors, so only purchase them if and when they're needed.

Breastfeeding bras

By now you've probably already bought maternity bras for your pregnancy, so you might be wondering why you need to cough up for another set. As with good maternity bras, breastfeeding bras should be supportive and adjustable – the crucial difference here is that the cups undo to allow easier access to the breast at feeding time. Additionally, your boobs might have expanded since early pregnancy and could become even more ample post-birth – breastfeeding bras are stretchy yet supportive, allowing for the size changes that can occur throughout the day and night in the postnatal period.

Do you really need them?

If you intend to breastfeed, then yes, as they make life easier and more comfortable. We recommend buying three (one on, one spare, one in the wash) but keep the packaging and receipts in case you need a different size or breastfeeding doesn't work out.

When?

Get fitted for breastfeeding bras after 36 weeks of your pregnancy – Marks & Spencer, John Lewis and the National Childbirth Trust offer fitting services. Don't get measured before then as there could still be last-minute changes to your body.

Look for:

- *wide straps* to add support and prevent cutting into your shoulders.
- *machine washable fabrics* – now is not the time for hand-washing lingerie.
- as much *cotton* as possible to help keep your boobs cool if they get engorged.
- *cups that are easy to undo* and do up again one-handed (you'll be holding your baby).
- *non-wired bras* as wires can cause breast lumps or mastitis in breast-feeding women.

Mothercare (pretty and well-priced), Elle Macpherson nursing bras (for those who want to splurge on something glam), Noppies bras (basic but comfortable).

Feeding pillows

These sound like a luxury but by improving positioning they can contribute significantly to whether breastfeeding is successful. If you're expecting twins and wish to breastfeed both simultaneously, they're essential.

Bottle-feeders will also find such pillows a useful way to get comfortable, position their baby and prevent poor posture while feeding. Some feeding pillows can double as an aid to comfortable sleeping in pregnancy and as a support when your baby is learning to sit later on.

Look for: *a washable, removable cover.*

'My Brest Friend' pillow – see below. For Twins, the EZ-2 Nurse Twins Pillow.

Product showcase – we're big fans of the My Brest Friend feeding pillow (despite the naff name). Unlike standard feeding cushions, it straps around you and has a flat top allowing the baby to lie comfortably without rolling down. It provides good lumbar support, prevents the cushion slipping and leaves your hands free to position your baby.

My Brest Friend pillow

Nipple cream

For mothers rather than babies but essential to soothe sore and cracked nipples.

Lansinoh (a favourite of breastfeeding experts), Motherlove Nipple Cream (lanolin-free), Biofem Nipple Balm (natural and lanolin-free).

Breastfeeding clothing

Tops and dresses specially designed for feeding aren't a necessity, as you can just wear regular clothes that provide easy access to your boobs at feeding time. The only exception is if you carry your baby in a sling a lot in which case breastfeeding clothing might be worthwhile.

Otherwise, if you feel the need to guard your modesty, you could drape a scarf, poncho or large muslin across yourself.

BABY BOTTLES

Feeding bottles used to be simple affairs – glass or plastic bottles with latex teats. Then, as with many other baby products, things got much more complicated, with 'anti-colic systems', 'variflow orthodontic teats', designer versions from the likes of Dior, and even a bottle that looks like a breast.

So, visit say Boots or Mothercare these days to buy bottles and it's easy to end up staring blankly at the huge selection, wondering which to choose. But we're here to get to the bottom of it all, starting with some basics.

Baby bottle terminology:

Teats – most teats (the soft bit the baby sucks on) nowadays are made from clear silicone, although some are the more traditional latex (yellowy rubber). Silicone is more durable and easier to clean whereas latex needs changing frequently as it can deteriorate over time. Latex however is natural, softer and more 'skin-like'. Some brands such as Nuk and Bibi offer a choice of latex or silicone teats, whereas the market leaders, Avent and Dr Brown, only produce silicone ones. You can sometimes use a different brand of teat on a specific bottle but watch out for leaks.

Flow rates – teats come in slow, medium, fast and variable flows. The rate and/or number of holes at the top determine how much milk the baby gets when sucking. Slow is usually best for newborns, medium from three to six months and fast from six months plus. If your baby gets frustrated or falls asleep mid-way through feeds, try a faster-flowing teat. Thicker, 'hungry baby' formula also requires faster flow teats. Variable flow versions offer several rates in one teat depending on which way up you put the bottle into the baby's mouth.

Anti-colic systems/valves – some bottles claim to reduce the amount of air taken in, preventing windiness and colic which can make babies unsettled. Manufacturers tout their own research to back these claims but given the lack of independent evidence and the fact no one really knows what causes colic, the jury is still out on this. That said, if you have a colicky baby, you'll probably go with any potential solution so such bottles are worth trying (cranio-sacral/osteopathic therapy sometimes works well in this situation).

How many?

This depends on how you'll feed your baby and as this doesn't always go as planned, you'll have to use your best guess.

If solely bottle-feeding: buy six (tiny babies typically have this many feeds daily so this allows you to only have to wash them once a day).

If mixed feeding (both breast and bottle with either expressed or formula milk): buy two for now and more if you increase bottle-feeds.

If breastfeeding only: buy two bottles just in case things don't work out or for giving expressed milk.

££ Dinky newborn-sized bottles (120-150ml) have a limited life as before you know it your baby will be guzzling feeds too big to fit in them. It's fine to use full-size bottles from the start – just ensure they come with newborn teats or purchase the correct teats separately.

Look for:

- *An appropriate teat* for your baby's stage – some bottles include newborn teats, some only faster flow ones; you can buy different teats separately if needed.
- *Ease of cleaning* – don't under-estimate the importance of this – you'll be scrubbing six bottles a day if you solely bottle-feed. Some brands have more components than others, making them harder to wash, assemble and fit in standard sterilisers. The otherwise excellent Dr Brown's are the worst culprits for this. Wide neck bottles are generally easier to clean (and to fill) than narrow necked ones.
- Check bottles are *dishwasher safe* (unless of course you don't have a dishwasher) – most are, provided they go on the top rack. Note though that frequent dishwashing could reduce bottles' lifespan by causing scratches (see page 61).

- *Bottle 'systems'* – allow you to convert bottles into trainer cups later on by adding toddler spouts and handles. These can be worthwhile, although your baby might not take to that brand's spout (even if they liked the bottles) so just buy one spout and see if your toddler accepts it before buying a full set.

- *Breastfeeding 'compatibility'* – if you're planning to mixed feed, choose a bottle that complements breastfeeding. Many lactation experts recommend Dr Brown's bottles for this, as the action required to 'milk' them is closest to milking a breast. BornFree bottles, relatively new to the UK, are similar to Dr Brown's in this respect but are bisphenol-A free plastic (see page 61) and easier to clean.

Steer clear of ...

- Choosing a bottle brand just because it integrates with a breast pump unless it is the breast pump you're sure you want. The risk is that either the breast pump won't be the best for you or the bottles won't be the best for your baby.

★ *Dr Brown's, BornFree, Tommee Tippee Closer to Nature.*

Specialist bottles

Specialist bottles, such as the Medela Haberman Feeder, are designed for premature babies or those with a sucking or palate problem. If this applies to your baby, seek advice from your consultant or health visitor. They can also be worth trying if you have a breastfed baby who is refusing standard bottles.

Disposable bottles

Single-use bottles mean no washing and sterilising when travelling. They take up a lot of luggage space on the outward journey and aren't very eco- friendly. Check before packing whether your baby will even accept a disposable bottle's teat if they're used to a different type. We're not keen on Playtex's system with disposable liners – they're popular in the US but you still have to wash the reusable teats and they can be fiddly to use.

Product showcase – Swiss firm Bibi makes a bio-degradable disposable bottle with a concertina design that packs down to half its normal size, folding out for use.

Bibi, Tommee Tippee Steri-bottles.

The 'eye-catching' Adiri Breastbottle

The unusual-looking Adiri Breastbottle resembles a breast and is intended to be softer and more acceptable to breastfed babies. They're worth trying for a baby who has refused every other bottle but can be a nightmare to fit into sterilisers (they're much wider than normal) and quite expensive. Their unusual shape is sure to make them a talking point at post-natal coffee mornings though.

Hands-free bottles – the Poddee

These curious contraptions are designed as 'hands-free' feeding bottles. The baby sucks on a teat attached to a flexible straw that leads into a bottle. The bottle can sit either on a nearby flat surface or in a holder strapped to a pushchair or baby seat. They're useful for bottle-feeding multiples simultaneously but being close to your baby (or babies) during feeds is one of parenting's joys, so this system shouldn't be overused or abused. Note that the straw component of the Poddee can only be cold water sterilised.

Steriliser bottles (see page 63)

There's concern that some plastic baby bottles (those made from polycarbonate plastic) can leach a substance called bisphenol-A, potentially disrupting babies' hormone levels. Recent studies suggest this is especially the case when such bottles are filled with boiling water. Experts are still divided on whether this poses a real risk to babies' health, but if it worries you, alternative plastic bottles, made from polypropelene, polyamide or silicone which do not contain bisphenol-A (BPA), are now available (e.g. BornFree, Mam, Babisil)

Glass bottles are also making a comeback and are the greenest option of all, albeit heavier to carry round and, of course, breakable. If you opt for regular plastic, we recommend replacing bottles that are scratched as chemicals such as BPA may be able to leach more easily.

BOTTLE-FEEDING ACCESSORIES

Bottle cleaning brushes

Help ensure thorough hand-washing, especially when milk gets dried into nooks and crannies. Cheap and worthwhile.

Flask

If you'll need to warm bottles at night or when out, an insulated flask will keep water hot for several hours – simply stand the bottle in the hot water for a few minutes. Better still, get your baby used to room-temperature milk so warming bottles won't be needed.

Insulated bottle holders

Some changing bags come with these included (again they're not needed if your baby accepts room-temperature milk). Otherwise wait and see if you need one.

Milk powder dispensers

Handy canisters to hold pre-measured formula portions when you're out. Mothercare, Avent and Tommee Tippee all make them.

Dishwasher baskets

These are cheap and although by no means essential, they keep bottle teats and smaller items from falling off the shelf onto the dishwasher element below where they might melt.

Bottlewarmers

Don't bother with these – they take too long! If you must warm milk, it's quicker to sit the bottle in hot water, either from the kettle or a flask.

Bottle drying racks

OK, they prevent bottles from tipping over, but what's wrong with a normal dish rack?

> **Parent panel tip:** "I keep in stock a few cartons of ready-made formula for when we're out. It's more expensive than powder but also very useful when I don't have any cooled boiled water or have run out of powder."

STERILISERS

Do you really need one?

Sterilisers are essential for bottle-feeding and for bowls and spoons during the first stages of weaning.

Whilst 'official' UK recommendations are to sterilise all feeding equipment until your baby is 12 months, many parents question how necessary this is once their baby is putting everything, clean or unclean into their teeny mouth.

In our opinion it is worth sticking with the guidelines and sterilising milk bottles throughout the first year as the white stuff provides an ideal breeding ground for bacteria. Yes, our American friends just use their dishwashers but many Brits don't have one or don't run theirs daily, which means washing bottles by hand in between. Sterilising provides extra reassurance that hand-washed bottles are germ-free.

You *can* sterilise equipment in a pan of boiling water for 10 minutes but it's a faff and as a sleep-deprived new parent, it's all too easy to accidentally leave the pan to boil dry, potentially ruining both the pan and its contents. We think it's worth investing in a proper unit – it will get plenty of use.

When do you need it?

If you think you'll bottle-feed early on, purchase a steriliser in advance of the birth. Otherwise you can wait and buy it if you introduce bottles or when you start weaning.

Look for:

- *A decent capacity* – what's needed depends on your feeding method. If you mainly or exclusively bottle-feed, you'll probably prefer to sterilise a full day's feeds at once – usually six bottles for a newborn. If you mainly breastfeed, this is less of an issue, but a decent-sized one will still be valuable so you can fit weaning bowls or a breast pump into it.

- *Speed* – waiting 12 minutes for the steriliser to finish while your baby screams for a feed because you forgot to switch it on is not a relaxing experience. The fastest steam sterilisers take five minutes, microwave ones take from two to eight minutes. Quicker is obviously better.

Steer clear of:

- Buying a steriliser because it includes some free bottles with it – the bottles might not be the best for your baby.

Types of steriliser

1 *Cold water* – this involves placing a chemical sterilising tablet or liquid into a large container of water and soaking the feeding equipment in it for at least 15 to 30 minutes, depending on the brand. It takes longer than other methods, smells quite unpleasant and some babies dislike the residual taste. You also need to remember to keep a stock of tablets/solution and to change the solution every 24 hours. Only worth considering if you have items that can only be cold water sterilised (this is rare) or if you are travelling and don't have access to a microwave or electric travel steriliser.

2 *Microwave* – convenient and more compact than electric alternatives, microwave sterilisers are simply glorified lidded plastic boxes. You place your feeding equipment and a measured amount of water into the tub, and bung it in the microwave for two to eight minutes, depending on the steriliser and your microwave's wattage. This last

point is key – certain manufacturers boast of sterilisation times of as little as two minutes, but if you look carefully this is for a super-powerful 1100 watt microwave – most newish domestic models are only around 700 to 900 watts, which would take four minutes. If your microwave is of very low wattage, you might be better off with an electric steam steriliser (or investing in a new microwave).

Many microwave sterilisers have a smaller capacity than electric ones – usually four bottles (although a few take six, including Avent's). If you exclusively bottle-feed a young baby on six feeds a day, smaller sterilisers won't allow you to do all the day's bottles at once, which could be annoying.

It sounds obvious but do check the steriliser will fit in your microwave before buying.

Microwave sterilisers are light to carry when travelling and although they're bulky, you can store bottles in them to use the space well. Unlike electric sterilisers they don't take so much space up on your kitchen work surfaces but note that some breast pumps and metal cutlery cannot be sterilised in a microwave (most weaning spoons are plastic so this isn't a big problem).

★ *Avent, Tommee Tippee, Dr Brown's.*

3 *Electric steam* – these are an effective choice if you plan to solely/mainly bottle-feed or have twins and will need to sterilise a lot of bottles daily. They have a kettle-style element which boils a small amount of water turning it into steam, which kills bacteria.

It's important to choose a model that's quick (the best take five to six minutes). Some newer steam sterilisers allow a continuous cycle to run, keeping contents sterile for 24hours but this isn't necessary –

we've never heard of a baby being harmed by unused bottles that were sterilised more than a few hours beforehand.

On the downside, electric sterilisers are bulky, taking up work surface space in the kitchen, and will need de-scaling periodically if you live in a hard water area, but if you'll bottle-feed a lot or don't own a microwave (or a decent-sized one), their convenience makes up for this.

★ *Avent electric sterilisers.*

Verdict: go for a large capacity microwave steriliser provided your microwave is big enough to take it and powerful enough to sterilise quickly. Otherwise choose an electric steam model with a quick cycle.

Product showcase – Mothercare Steriliser Bottles can be sterilised in the microwave on a stand-alone basis – you don't need any other equipment (they can also be sterilised using other methods). This is the fastest way to sterilise a small number of bottles, taking only 90 seconds for one (although that rises to 6.5 minutes for six). We're not too keen on these as firstly there are better baby bottles on the market and also if you want to sterilise weaning bowls and spoons later on, you'll have to buy another form of steriliser.

Travel sterilisers

Steriliser bags are superbly convenient when you're away from home if you'll have access to a microwave. You simply shove one or two washed bottles into the bag, pour a little water in and put it in the microwave for three minutes. They pack away to virtually nothing and can be reused up to 20 times, but since they only take two bottles at a time they aren't suitable for everyday use.

Another portable option is Babytec's travel electric steam steriliser which is quick and easy to use. It only takes two bottles at a time but we recommend it for travelling if no microwave is available.

★ *Babytec electric travel steriliser, Lindam or Medela microwave bags.*

WEANING EQUIPMENT AND TRAINING CUPS

Introducing solid foods is a small but exciting step on your baby's path towards growing up. When to first offer solids is a surprisingly contentious issue. Current 'official' recommendations are to wait until six months but many parents struggle to hold off this long when faced with a hungry baby keenly showing an interest in devouring something other than milk. It's wise to discuss early weaning with your health visitor or GP.

When do you need it?

Even if you introduce solids a little earlier than the official guideline of six months, it's unlikely you'll need weaning gear before four to five months.

What do you need?

Spoons

The feel of a spoon in a young baby's mouth can be quite alien to them and the type used when weaning can make a difference to how well they accept solids initially. Soft-tipped spoons are better than harder ones for the early days.

You can manage with two or three, but more means you won't have to wash up every mealtime. Later on you can introduce firmer plastic or metal spoons.

Initially: Vital Baby soft-tipped weaning spoons. Later on: Tommee Tippee spoon multipacks.

Storage tubs and cubes

For keeping homemade baby food in the fridge or freezer. Many parents batch cook puréed food, freeze it and defrost small amounts as needed. Of course you can use any pots but the smaller ones for baby food allow greater flexibility and reduce waste as you only need to defrost the appropriate portion each time.

Ice cube trays are especially good for freezing purées – the soft silicone ones make it easier to pop out the portions. We also like the individual cubes with lids ('weaning cubes'). Brother Max Food Portioners are especially good – the individual cubes click together and snap apart easily, can be microwaved and are very easy to pop frozen food out of.

Brother Max Food Partitioners, Happy Mummy Baby Cubes, Beaba multi-portion trays.

Plates and bowls

Babies chuck things on the floor, sometimes on purpose, sometimes by accident. You needn't choose specific baby/toddler dishes with kiddy characters but something unbreakable is wise.

Bowls are better than plates for older babies who are self-feeding, as they can scoop things up more easily against the high sides. Look for crockery that can go in the microwave, freezer and dishwasher for convenience.

Having a couple of sealable containers is worthwhile if you'll take home-made baby food out with you.

Baby Bjorn 'First Bowl and Spoon' set, Ikea's bargain cheap, brightly-coloured kids' range, First Years.

> **Product showcase** – a cheap and cheerful way to stop toddlers tipping their snacks on the floor, The Snack Trap is a little bowl with a flexible sectioned lid. It allows small fingers to reach in and grab food but stops contents falling out if it's turned upside down.
>
> *snack trap*

Weaning bibs

When your baby is tiny, soft towelling or cotton bibs adequately soak up milk spills and dribble but with solid food something more robust is required to help prevent changes of clothing due to errant carrot purée.

Either go for something wipe-able with a food-catching pocket at the bottom or, for maximum protection, long-sleeved bibs. The latter also work well for messy toddler activities like finger painting. Buy three or four – they're a little more expensive than standard bibs but one size should last from weaning through to around age two.

Tommee Tippee Roll n Go, Kooshies, Baby Bjorn coveralls, Silly Billyz long-sleeved bibs.

Baby food processors

We have mixed feelings on these mini food processors, designed to help in preparation of purées. Some parents (including one of us!) think highly of the Beaba Baby Cook, which steams, blends, defrosts and reheats babyfood in one machine. It saves on washing up, and helps avoid worries about burns from hotspots in microwaved food. If you're planning on making homemade purées then this could be a worthwhile purchase but it is expensive at £65, and will only be useful for a shortish period. It certainly isn't a 'must-have' and a hand blender is a cheaper alternative which can be used for adult recipes and baby purées alike.

Beaba Babycook

Gripper/suction mats

These suction baby bowls onto the table/highchair tray, the idea being to reduce the chances of spills or the baby chucking bowl plus contents on the floor. Whilst they might prevent some incidents, they aren't strong enough to stop more determined toddlers pulling the bowls off and so we think they aren't worthwhile.

Recipe books

If you'll make your own baby food, a baby recipe book might provide inspiration although of course advice and recipes are available for free on the internet.

> ★ *Annabel Karmel's Baby and Toddler Meal Planner, The Food Doctor for Babies and Children.*

TIP: if you don't like the idea of jarred baby food but haven't the energy to cook constantly, companies such as Truly Scrumptious, Fresh Daisy and So Baby offer freezer packs of baby purées. They're much the same as if you made them yourself, with absolutely no additives or extras and many of the brands are organic.

TRAINING CUPS

By around age one, it's recommended you stop using baby bottles and move on to 'training' or 'spouty' cups. In reality, many babies struggle to adapt to these, so don't worry if yours is a little older when they give up their bottles. You might have to try several brands to identify one your baby likes, so only buy one initially. When you've worked out which suits your baby, you'll need two or three more.

Tommee Tippee Easiflow, Avent Magic Cups, Dr Brown's Trainer Cup, BornFree (bisphenol-A free) trainer cups. For younger babies try the Tommee Tippee First Cup.

HIGHCHAIRS

From weaning until your baby is big enough and sensible enough to sit in a grown-up chair, a highchair will be a major feature of your kitchen. Choose the style wisely and you needn't wince at some garish monstrosity on a daily basis. It's crucial that it's easy to clean – whether you go for cheap and cheerful or swanky and pricey, it *will* get covered in gunk on an all too regular basis.

Do you really need one?

You need some sort of chair to feed your baby in although it doesn't have to be a conventional highchair – see page 187.

When do you need it?

Not before weaning (around four to six months) and even then for the first couple of months of giving solids, you could use a bouncy chair or 'Bumbo' type seat (see page 180), delaying purchasing a highchair until your baby reaches six to seven months old.

The main buying decisions:

2 'Proper' highchair or portable seat?

The majority of parents purchase a proper highchair but you can make do with a combination of a bouncy chair for the early, 'spoon-feeding' days and then a cheaper booster seat or portable highchair once your baby can sit at the table and doesn't need so much support. This saves money as you'll probably be buying a bouncy chair anyway (see page

178), plus the portable highchair takes up less space and can be used away from home.

First Years and Safety First's versions cost around £25 and Argos have a perfectly decent one with a tray for £15. More stylish is the HandySitt – it's wood rather than bright plastic and it's easier to clean than the others although it is more expensive. For more on portable highchairs, see page 187.

2 Wood or plastic/metal?

Wooden highchairs have staged a comeback in recent years as a more attractive alternative to plastic and metal versions. Metal highchair manufacturers have in turn upped the style ante with funkier designs that are more pleasing on the eye.

Wooden models tend to have fewer nooks and crannies for food to lodge in so are easier to clean, although they can be less comfortable and supportive for younger babies unless you add a cushion. Some wooden highchairs convert into adult chairs later on (see page 73).

Stokke Tripp Trapp (wooden, no tray, converts to adult chair), Svan (wooden, removable tray, converts to adult chair), Fresco Bloom highchair (super-cool, no nooks and crannies but super-expensive too), Chicco Polly, Mamas and Papas' Prima Pappa, Cosatto Aurora (all stylish 'fully-featured' metal models).

3 Tray or no tray?

Highchairs can have a fixed tray, a removable one or no tray.

Trayless models are used up at the dining table, the idea being that your baby learns about eating techniques and table manners earlier because they're more 'integrated' into family meals. We buy into this philosophy and believe it works, but if you prefer to contain mess (as far as you can) or have a particularly precious dining table, a tray might be wise.

A highchair with a removable tray gives you the choice of your baby/toddler sitting at the table or not and allows you to start off with the tray for a young baby but remove it at the toddler stage.

Svan (has a removable tray).

4 Do you want it to last beyond the baby stage?

Some highchairs are more adjustable than others and are roomy enough for older toddlers. Some (usually wooden ones) convert to adult chairs later on. Overall, convertible highchairs tend to be pricier and are only worthwhile if you actually like the style of the chair they become (although our recommended options are excellent highchairs anyway).

Stokke Tripp Trapp or the Svan (both convert to adult chairs).

5 Does it need to fold?

If space is tight in your kitchen, consider a highchair which folds up when not in use. Plastic/metal models usually do, although check the folded dimensions as some fold more compactly than others. Basic highchairs are often better for this than 'all-singing' ones. The Tripp Trapp is particularly slim even though it doesn't fold and is as compact as many that do. Another option is to go with the 'bouncy chair followed by booster seat' combination mentioned above.

Cosatto's On The Move, Tripp Trapp.

Look for:

Essential:

- *Easy cleaning* – avoid anything with lots of nooks and crannies that food will lodge in. Look for smooth surfaces that will be easy to wipe down.
- *Adjustability* – so that the highchair will suit your baby from early weaning through to when they're ready to sit on a proper chair.
- *Easy access* – you need to be able to get your baby in and out of the highchair easily. Check whether the tray (if there is one) will get in the way or can be moved aside, pulled outwards or lifted off with ease.
- *A supportive seat* – in the early stages of weaning you'll need the highchair to be supportive so your baby feels comfortable and secure. Some models have a cushion (included or at extra cost) to help with this. It's crucial that the cushion is washable or wipeable as it's going to get seriously messy.
- *A 'crotch' bar* that sits between the baby's legs to prevent slipping down. If there's no bar you will definitely need to use a harness (with a bar some people feel it's safe not to as you should always supervise a baby in a highchair anyway). We aren't big fans of harnesses (they're fiddly to open, a nightmare if a baby is choking and difficult to clean) so favour highchairs with crotch bars.
- *An integral harness or d-rings* to attach one to – as mentioned above, you will definitely need this if there is no crotch bar. Although we prefer trying to avoid harnesses, if you end up with a particularly adventurous toddler who tries to climb out of their highchair, you'll have no choice but to add one to prevent accidents.
- *A design that you can live with* – because this highchair is going to sit in your kitchen for at least the next couple of years. Conversely don't, of course, be seduced by style alone.

Useful:

- *Castors* – some highchairs are quite heavy so castors will be helpful if you will move it around a lot, say between a kitchen and dining room.

Don't pay extra for:

- *A recline feature* – you really don't need this.
- *Integral toy tidies* – unnecessary and another place for food thrown/dropped off the highchair to gather.

> **Product showcase** – Ikea Antilop highchair – it's inoffensive looking, extremely easy to clean, very portable (you can quickly remove the legs and shove them plus the seat in the car to take to the grandparents), and it's as cheap as the chips your toddler will want to eat in it. At £11.99, this is one of the best baby bargains around (it's all of £3 extra for the optional tray). It's also especially good for twins – two 'normal' highchairs cost a fortune and take up a lot of space, whereas Antilops can be stacked on top of each other.
>
> ★ *Idea Antlop highchair*

DUMMIES (also known as soothers)

Not strictly feeding gear, but as well as being a sleeping aid and comforter, dummies can be a useful alternative to the breast for 'sucky' babies in between feeds and they do go in the mouth, after all. They're controversial little things, with countless debates about their pros and cons. It's an entirely personal decision as to whether you want your baby to have one or not.

If you do, orthodontic soothers are preferable to round/cherry-shaped ones as they're less likely to damage a baby's teeth and jaw formation, although some parents find the cherry ones stay in babies' mouths better. Clear silicone teats last longer than latex (the yellowy rubber) but latex feels more skin-like, so might be acceptable to babies who've rejected silicone. If your baby develops a favourite dummy, buy spares as they tend to get lost.

TIP: if your baby has a dummy, buy a 'soother saver' to clip it to your baby's clothes, preventing it from falling on the floor and getting grubby.

6

Sleeping – first beds and the nursery

Shopping list

✓ Cot/cot-bed plus mattress

✓ Storage – drawers, wardrobe or both

✓ A comfortable chair for feeding

? Smaller first bed such as a Moses basket, plus mattress

? Changing unit

? Blackout curtains or blinds

? Nursery decoration

(Bedding is discussed on pages 102–17)

If the most precious thing in a new parent's life is their baby, you can bet the second most precious thing will be sleep. Sit with any group of new parents and it'll almost certainly be a hot topic of conversation.

The short-term goal is to attain the Holy Grail of '*sleeping through the night*'. Of course, how long it's going to be before you get a vaguely decent night's sleep won't be determined solely by where your baby sleeps or what they sleep in, but such things can make life a little easier during this most exhausting of times.

The early days (and nights)

Guidelines from The Foundation for the Study of Infant Deaths (FSID) say the safest place for a baby to sleep at night during their first six months is in your bedroom (but not in your bed). Bedroom sharing also makes night feeds slightly more bearable, with no stumbling across a chilly, dark hallway at 3am. Be warned though that newborns might be small but they can be disproportionately noisy sleepers and disturbing each other can be a problem. How long you stick it out before packing your little one off to the nursery is up to you – for some it feels right to room-share for years, for others it's a relief to no longer hear every snore, groan or moan their baby makes.

New babies sleep a lot (frustratingly not always when you want them to) so think about where yours will nap in the day, and whether you want a portable first bed so you can keep a close eye on them, or are happy to be in different rooms, perhaps using a baby monitor for reassurance.

FIRST BEDS (Moses baskets, carrycots, cribs and hammocks)

Many parents choose a smaller first sleeping place for their newborn, usually a Moses basket, carrycot or crib, before moving on to a proper cot later. Not yet mainstream but growing in popularity are baby hammocks.

When budgeting, consider that these smaller beds will be outgrown quickly as within three or four months and certainly by six months, most babies need a proper cot. Also, factor in the cost of an extra set of smaller bedding – sheets, mattress protectors and blankets.

Do you really need one?

Strictly speaking, no. It's perfectly safe for a newborn to sleep in a full-size cot from day one but tiny babies look, and possibly feel, rather lost in one. After being tightly cosseted in your mum's tum, sleeping in a cot must be the equivalent of an adult bedding down for the night on the pitch at Wembley Stadium – not exactly cosy.

Crucially, if your baby starts off sleeping in your bedroom (most newborns do), a smaller first bed takes up considerably less floor space and if you choose a portable option (a carrycot or Moses basket), you can cart your slumbering newborn around the house with you.

When do you need it?

As soon as your baby gets home from hospital.

How to decide?

In order to work out which option is best for you and your baby, think carefully about the following:

- Do you want to keep your newborn close during daytime naps as well as at night? If so, choose a Moses basket or carrycot rather than a crib.
- Is space very limited in your bedroom (assuming your baby will sleep in there at first)? If so a smaller first bed will be particularly valuable.
- How much can you afford to/do you want to spend on something that will only be used for a few months? Moses baskets are usually cheaper than cribs and carrycots.

- Do you plan more children and want something durable so are therefore willing to spend more?

FIRST BEDS – an overview

	Moses baskets	**Cribs**	**Carrycots**	**Hammocks**	**Cot or cot-bed from birth**
Typical cost	£40–£100 incl. mattress	£50+ to £150+ mattress (£10–£45)	£100 to £170 incl. mattress	£40–£150+ incl. mattress	You'll be buying one anyway so it isn't an extra expense
Extra bedding needed	Yes	Yes	Yes	Yes	No
Easy to reach from your bed	Only with a stand (around £20)	Yes	Only with a stand (around £20)	Depends on model	Only if there is a drop side
Portability	Good	Poor	Good	Depends on model	Poor
Rocking motion or movement	Only with a rocking stand	Depends on the model	Only with a rocking stand	Yes	No
Lasts until:	3–4 mths	4–6 mths	4–6 mths	6–9 months depending on the model	2.5–3 years (longer for cot-beds)

Other pros

CARRYCOTS – Multi-purpose – can be used on the pram

COT OR COT-BED FROM BIRTH – No worries about transferring baby to a cot later

Other cons

CARRYCOTS – Second mattress needed if the original is unsuitable for overnight sleeping

HAMMOCKS – Potential for dependence on motion to get to sleep, causing problems when transferred to a normal cot

COT OR COT-BED FROM BIRTH – Take up more floor space and some newborns feel lost in a full cot.

Types of first bed:

1 Moses baskets

For some parents, these little woven baskets, dressed up with valances and canopies fulfil a sentimental vision of a newborn's bed. For this reason, you might decide you've got to have one.

Looking solely at practicalities though, their value is less clear-cut. Yes, they're compact and more portable than a crib but actually some people find them awkward to carry. They can be taken to friends' or relatives' houses but you might want to buy a travel cot anyway so could use that instead. Also, be warned that inexplicably some babies particularly hate Moses baskets – one mum we know so much as put her little bundle in his and he'd have a meltdown. (Mind you, this was the same fussy chap whose parents became so desperate to get him to sleep at 3am one night that his dad drove him round the entire M25.)

The biggest criticism of Moses baskets is that they're so small they're usually outgrown by three months, although obviously if you have subsequent children, you will get more use out of it. Certainly if the pram you want comes with a detachable carrycot, you can avoid buying a Moses basket too as, fundamentally, they do the same job.

Verdict: good for the first few weeks, portable and compact but don't spend a fortune as it won't be used for long (or borrow one, buying a new mattress for as little as £10).

Look for:

Essential:

- A *removable, washable lining.*
- A basket *lining that isn't too padded* – FSID's advice is that it should be thin to reduce the risk of overheating.
- A *sturdy basket.*
- Comfortable to hold, *secure handles.*
- A *firm mattress* (mattresses are nearly always included with Moses baskets).

Useful:

- A *stand* –these aren't essential but keep the basket at a convenient height next to your bed. Some parents place the basket into their baby's cot instead but this only really works if you buy the cot early enough and have room in your bedroom for it, or are putting the baby to sleep in its own room from birth (which is not recommended by experts).

  If you do buy a stand and it rocks, check it can also be fixed in position (some babies love being rocked to sleep, others don't).

2 Cribs

Remember that song 'You say tomayto, I say tomarto, you say patayto, I say potarto …'? Well, when it comes to baby kit, Brits and Americans do indeed talk different languages. In the US, cribs are what we Brits call cots, whereas over here a crib is what they call a cradle – a 'mini' cot suitable for a newborn's first few months.

So, to clarify, we're talking Brit terminology here. Some cribs are suspended so they swing, others have shaped, 'rocking' feet like the base of a rocking chair, others don't move at all. Motion sends most babies to sleep but check the crib can also be locked into a fixed position if yours dislikes it. Remember also that once your baby moves into a cot, you won't be able to rock him or her so if they're used to being rocked to sleep, you might be storing up trouble for later.

The crib will be at a similar height to your bed and as you can see through the side bars, you can check on your baby without having to lean over the side – helpful for mums with stitches from a c-section or in unspeakable places. However, cribs aren't portable, so if you want your baby nearby in the day, you'll need somewhere else for naps downstairs (if you live in a flat or bungalow, then a crib on castors could be wheeled between rooms). If your budget allows, a crib for night-time and a pram carrycot for daytime naps works well *(see combinations below).*

As cribs are that bit bigger, they have a slightly longer useful life than Moses baskets – manufacturers and retailers usually say up to six months although in reality most babies go into a cot by four or five months. Note, this won't save you money, as you'll need a cot anyway, albeit a month or two later than with a Moses basket or carrycot.

If a traditional, 'fairytale' look is your thing, drapes and canopies can be added to cribs. Your baby will be too young to care how flouncy their crib is, so these are purely decorative and really for your benefit not theirs.

If co-sleeping with your baby appeals but you are worried about the risks, bedside cribs are worth considering (see page 87).

Look for:

- A crib that can be *locked in position if it rocks.*

Also consider:

- The cost of a mattress (if not included with crib).

- The size of mattress needed (ensure it's a snug fit for safety).

3 Carrycots

If you're buying a pram with a removable carrycot (see page 120) you can skip the Moses basket or crib and use this instead. Some parents prefer the more contemporary look of carrycots to the frillier style of Moses baskets anyway and they're usually more robust too.

The biggest advantage of a carrycot though is multi-functionality – you'll get plenty of use out of it – and if your newborn falls asleep in the pram while you're out walking (many reliably doze off with a combination of fresh air and movement), you can unclamp the carrycot and bring it into the living room.

Carrycots can be moved around the house easily and used for overnight sleeping provided the mattress is appropriate – some are too soft or may not be sufficiently 'breathable' for a full night's use. Check with the retailer and if necessary buy an extra mattress for night-time – foam carrycot mattresses cost between £10 and £20. (See page 94–95).

The lifespan of a carrycot will be from birth to around six months for use on the pram but by four or five months it might be too cramped for overnight use.

At night, you can keep the carrycot at a similar height to your bed using a Moses basket stand but carrycots are bigger than Moses baskets so it can be difficult to find one that fits (the Mamas & Papas rocking stand works for most carrycots).

Overall, carrycots can be expensive and certainly if you aren't buying one for your pram, a Moses basket will be cheaper. If you are buying a carrycot for the pram, they're much of a muchness so focus on the pram's features rather than the carrycot's. Some carrycots are 'car-compatible', but on the whole we don't recommend their use in cars due to safety concerns – see page 156).

Look for:

- A *removable, washable lining.*
- A *lining that isn't too padded* – FSID's advice is that it should be thin to reduce the risk of overheating.
- Comfortable to hold and *secure handles.*
- A *firm mattress suitable for overnight sleeping* (if the one that's included isn't, then an extra won't cost much).
- A *carrycot that detaches easily from the pram* – especially for when the baby is asleep in it as you won't want to wake them.

4 Full size cot or cot-bed from birth

The cheapest option of all is to use a cot or cot-bed from birth. Not only will you save money by not buying more than one 'bed', you can also avoid coughing up for the relevant smaller bedding that would only be used for a few months. Bedside cots (see page 87) are especially good for newborns as they can be pushed flush to your bed with no barrier between you and your baby, making night feeds easier and aiding bonding.

Cots obviously can't be moved around easily so if you prefer to keep your baby nearby at all times, you'll need somewhere else for them to nap when you aren't in the bedroom.

One possibility is to try your newborn in the cot and if they really hate it, go and buy a Moses basket – most baby stores keep a selection in stock.

For more on choosing cots/cot-beds, see page 88–91.

5 Hammocks

A small but growing number of parents are opting for a baby hammock as their newborn's first bed.

There are three main types:

- 'conventional' – suspended at both ends from a stand, like miniature versions of those garden hammocks you can buy in the likes of Homebase and B&Q.
- Cocoon-style – these have a little mattress that sits in a cocoon-like hammock suspended via a single hook from a doorframe or stand. The two best-known models are the Amby Nature's Nest and Moffii Cradle.
- The Leander Cradle – a Danish product that looks a little like a suspended carrycot, attached via a single hook to either the ceiling (you'll have to ensure yours is strong enough) or a wooden tripod stand.

The fundamental idea here is that baby hammocks lull babies to sleep by providing multi-directional movement similar to that in the womb. They're also designed to be gently supportive of a baby's spine.

We've heard of many babies who sleep like a dream in hammocks, but not all take to them (although not all babies like cots or Moses baskets either). Fear not if you do buy one and your baby hates it, as there's strong second-hand demand so you should recover much of your money on the likes of eBay.

Consider though that when your baby moves to a proper cot or cot-bed, you could be in for a rough time if they're used to the hammock's movement to rock them to sleep. Also some hammocks are marketed as being suitable sleeping places up to 12 months but we've found most parents stop using theirs once their baby can sit up and move around (by six to nine months). Even if they do last longer than a Moses basket or crib, this won't save you money as you'll need a cot anyway – just a bit later.

Overall, hammocks are best viewed as an alternative to a Moses basket, carrycot or crib – not as a longer-term replacement for a cot. Some people think they were key to their newborn's great sleeping habits, others wish they had bought something more conventional. Take some of the manufacturers' claims with a pinch of salt, and decide what appeals to you.

Moffii Cradle, Amby Nature's Nest.

'Bedside' cribs and cots are a wonderful solution if sharing your bed with your baby appeals (research suggests this helps prolong breastfeeding), but you're worried about the risk of smothering or overheating. One side of the crib or cot drops down (although it can be raised if it needs to 'stand alone' sometimes) and the base adjusts level with your mattress, forming a 'private wing' of the bed for your baby. Bedside cribs aren't widely sold but if you hunt around there are a few available. Check whether it will be compatible with your style of bed as some are designed to clip on to bedstead frames and therefore won't work with a divan.

Bedside cots don't come as part of a co-ordinated 'room set', so if later on you move it to the nursery and you want matching furniture such as a changing unit and wardrobe, you'll have to do your best to find something that works.

'Arms Reach Co-sleeper' cribs, Global Nursery Products bedside crib, Mamas & Papas / Cosatto bedside cots.

Combinations

If you buy and/or borrow wisely or have a generous budget, you could have more than one first sleeping place such as a cot or crib upstairs and a carrycot, Moses basket or hammock downstairs. This could help your baby differentiate between day and night earlier.

MOVING ON TO THE COT OR COT-BED

Whether your baby sleeps in it from birth or uses a smaller 'bed' initially, sooner or later you're going to need a cot or cot-bed. Most babies spend more time in their cot than anywhere else and the cot contributes significantly to the look of the nursery, so it's worth investing a bit of time in making a choice, both features and appearance wise.

If you want a cot/cot-bed that comes as part of a matching range of nursery furniture and decide you want a drop-side (see 89–90) or prefer a cot-bed to a cot, start with this premise rather than finding a range you love and then realising that it only has a cot not a cot-bed, or sides are fixed, not drop.

When do you need it?

Many cots/cot-beds will be available almost immediately, but some take up to twelve weeks to be delivered from ordering. If you'll use a Moses basket, carrycot or crib from birth, your baby won't need the cot until they're three or four months old, or more, but it's worth doing your research pre-baby if possible.

The main buying decisions:

Cot or cot-bed?

To the uninitiated they look broadly the same, so what's the difference?

- Cot-beds have slightly larger internal dimensions than cots – typically 140 x 70cm compared to 120 x 60cm for a standard cot.

- By removing its sides, the cot-bed converts into a 'junior' bed later on. This might last your child until age five or six, whereas a cot is normally outgrown (or escaped from – a common trigger for moving a toddler into a bed) by two-and-a-half to three. Cot-beds make a familiar stepping-stone between a cot and a single bed.

- Expense – generally cot-beds cost more than cots. Don't be fooled into thinking a cot-bed will save you money as you'll have to buy a single bed for your child sooner or later.

Verdict: the decision probably boils down to how much space you have and cost. If space isn't an issue, a cot-bed will generally be better than a cot as it eases the transition to a proper bed.

Look for:

Essential:

- At least *two different mattress heights.* Most models have two or three base positions. You need two – high for a newborn so taking them in/out is easier, and low for when they can sit up, to prevent babies flinging themselves over the side. Further positions aren't necessary and changing the base height is an extra job you probably won't want to do too often.

- A *durable material* – poorer quality veneer can chip, especially with a toddler bashing toys against it on a regular basis. Solid wood will last longer (especially relevant if you want to use the same cot/cot-bed for any subsequent babies).

Useful:

- *A drop-side* with a *quiet mechanism* that's *operable one-handed.*

This means one or both cot sides can be lowered, making it easier to get your baby in and out. This isn't an issue for newborns (at that stage you can keep the mattress base high up so you don't have to bend over the cot side). However, once the mattress is lowered to stop older babies climbing out, a drop-side is better for your back and indeed essential if you're prone to backache or are short, as bending over the cot side can be a strain. A drop-side also allows you to put an already sleeping baby in bed more gently, with less likelihood of them waking.

Some work with catches, others foot pedals – test them out. If the mechanism is noisy, it might jolt your sleeping baby awake. It really isn't an advantage if both sides drop, as the cot will probably be against a wall.

- An integral *teething rail* – many teething babies like to gnaw on the cot rail which can cause the wood to deteriorate, damaging the cot but probably not your baby. Some cot side rails are covered with non-toxic plastic 'teething rails'. Separate stick-on teething guards can be bought relatively cheaply (Prince Lionheart make them), so if the cot you've set your heart on doesn't have them, don't be put off. Be warned though that these stick-on rails won't fit on cots with unusually wide rims.
- *Castors* – these are valuable if you'll move the cot between rooms (check the cot will fit through your doorframes). They also make moving the cot easier when cleaning. The wheels must be lockable for safety reasons.

Steer clear of:

- Play features – a few cots feature integral 'playbeads', wooden beads that twirl around. These shouldn't influence your choice either way as more interesting toys are available that can be safely attached to a cot.

⚠ Cots and cot-beds should conform to the safety standard BS-EN 716-1. The bars must be no more than 45mm apart and the mattress should have a low base position. New cots in reputable stores will comply with regulations but second-hand ones and family hand-me-downs might not. The gap between the mattress and cot sides should be less than 4cm. Too tight a fit will make changing bedding difficult so a small gap is best.

Product showcase – the 'Stokke Sleepi' is that distinctive oval-shaped 'cot' you might see in some shops and which, depending on which add-ons you buy, starts off as a crib, converts to a cot and then to a junior bed. If that isn't enough multi-tasking, once the junior bed is outgrown, the Sleepi becomes two chairs or a sofa.

It's very well constructed from solid beech wood and, unlike other cots, needn't be consigned to gather dust in the loft when it's outgrown. Negatives are that the sides don't drop, and the kits needed to convert it from one 'form' into another cost extra so the 'multi-purposeness' is costly. In fact, if you buy the full shebang from crib to junior bed, it comes in at around £750, although that includes mattresses.

MATTRESSES

Manufacturers have upped the ante with baby mattresses in recent years, introducing fancy new materials and terminology and mentions of SIDS prevention. Perhaps it won't surprise you to learn that whilst a perfectly adequate standard sprung cot-bed mattress costs around £70, one boasting extra breathability, temperature controlling features, super-duper air flow functions and so on, can set you back at least double that.

In our opinion, and indeed that of many SIDS experts, there's a fair bit of playing on the fears of expectant parents going on. These premium mattresses are no safer than good quality standard ones. In fact, if we're talking purely about safety, there are just two unbreakable rules for baby mattresses (whether they are for use in cots or smaller first beds):

They must be firm (tiny babies can suffocate if they end up face down in a soft mattress)

They should fit snugly, with a gap of less than 4cm around each edge

Another thing to flag here is the importance of buying a new mattress. This isn't just a view peddled by the nursery industry to boost sales – FSID advises that ideally every baby should have a new mattress. If this isn't possible only use an old one if you know its history and it has a completely waterproof cover with no tears, cracks or holes in it. Clean and dry it thoroughly before use.

Look for:

Essential:

- *Firmness*
- A *snug fit* in the cotMosess basket/carrycot.

Useful:

- A *waterproof barrier* – if your baby does one of the dreaded four Ps (pee, poo, posset and puke) in the night, you'll be thankful for a waterproof barrier between the mattress and bedding, allowing you to clean up and get back to bed more quickly. If one of these yucky substances soaks into the mattress, it can take ages to dry out and soggy, unclean mattresses harbour bacteria. A mattress with an integral waterproof cover is useful but you can easily add one (see page 111). Waterproof covers should be breathable; the most basic PVC ones aren't and can get clammy in hot weather, potentially contributing to a baby over-heating. Some mattresses have waterproof material on one side and cotton on the other, the cotton side designed for use in summer and the wipe-able side for the rest of the time. Babies get sick in hot weather too, sometimes without warning, and you can bet the very night you turn the mattress over to the cotton side, your baby will develop a bout of vomiting.

- A *hypo-allergenic mattress* (if you're concerned about allergies) – an alternative is to use a mattress 'casing' that's impermeable to dust mites (their faeces contribute to allergies) and is also waterproof.

A word about PVC

In the mid-1990s there were concerns about links between PVC mattress covers and cot death – the theory being that when babies' urine makes contact with fire retardants used to treat PVC, toxic compounds are released that contribute to cot death. This theory has now largely been discounted by experts, but most manufacturers still make a big deal about using non-PVC materials for waterproof mattress coverings.

Organic and natural mattresses

In the UK, all mattresses, other than those made of naturally fire-retardant materials such as lambswool, must be treated with fire-retardant chemicals. At the time of writing, the Baby Products Association (BPA) is campaigning for baby mattresses to be exempt from fire-proofing but for now they aren't. We aren't aware of any scientific evidence to suggest fire retardants are harmful but if you prefer to limit the number of chemicals your baby is in contact with, you can buy 100% natural mattresses from specialist retailers such as Natural Mat Company.

Awkward sizes

If your baby's sleeping place isn't a standard size, most nursery retailers can order tailor-made or 'special-cut' mattresses. These won't usually cost much more but you'll need to allow extra time, as they can take three or four weeks to be made. For a crib or carrycot which needs a mattress with rounded corners or oval ends, we recommend providing the retailer with a template made from newspaper, so that you get the right shape.

The main buying decision:

Foam, sprung or natural?

1 *Foam*

Foam mattresses are relatively cheap and the most basic will simply be a chunk of foam encased in a plastic cover. More sophisticated versions have vents within the foam, usually around the middle and top. Note that if they're only at the top they will be fairly useless if the baby is sleeping in the recommended 'feet to foot position'. The ventilation holes are sometimes covered in mesh and intended to make the mattress more breathable to prevent clamminess or overheating, and to allow moisture such as sweat or regurgitated milk to drain away from the baby.

This sounds sensible but FSID suggests vents make a mattress harder to clean and does not recommend them. One idea is to use a breathable waterproof mattress cover over them – cleanliness shouldn't be a problem and the vents might still be beneficial.

Some pricier foam mattresses have a removable top layer of washable, breathable material making them less clammy and easier to keep clean as this can be put in the washing machine.

- ⊕ Cheaper than sprung interior or natural fibre, so particularly good for Moses baskets, carrycots and cribs that might only be used for a matter of weeks.
- ⊕ Lightweight, so easier to change bedding.
- ⊕ Non-allergenic as dust mites can't survive in foam.
- ⊖ Cheaper, thinner mattresses can sag and are not as comfortable for older babies as other options.
- ⊖ Must be kept covered with a waterproof layer to prevent bacteria growth.

2 *Sprung*

These contain a layer of springs, usually encased in foam or coir (natural coconut fibre) and sometimes other materials such as lambswool. Covers can be waterproof, PVC (or similar) or heavyweight cotton.

- ⊕ More comfortable and supportive than foam for older children (better for cot-beds).
- ⊖ More expensive than foam.
- ⊖ Heavier, so making the bed can be harder work – especially an issue if you've had a caesarean section.

3 *Coir*

Coir (natural coconut fibre) is a traditional mattress material. Sometimes it is sandwiched with natural latex, lambswool, or both. Coir mattresses tend to have natural cotton covers and therefore you'll need to buy a separate waterproof mattress protector (see page 111). This is a popular material in the 'greener' mattresses sold by organic baby products specialists.

- ⊕ Usually all natural so appealing for parents concerned about chemicals.

⊕ Supportive and long-lasting – keeps shape well and less likely to sag so especially good for a cot-bed which might be used for up to six years.

⊖ Expensive.

⊖ Not widely available in high street stores.

Verdict: for your baby's cot or cot-bed we suggest investing in a good quality coir or sprung mattress. For a first bed that might only see a couple of months' use or is only for naps, foam should suffice.

Look for:

- A *breathable but waterproof cover.* If it isn't waterproof, buy a separate mattress protector.
- *A mattress that isn't too heavy* – very heavy mattresses mean bed-making will be hard work.
- For foam mattresses, *foam that's thick* enough to provide sufficient support and comfort for the baby – at least 8cm in depth for a cot/cot-bed.

★ *Natural Mat Company and Rochingham.*

NURSERY STORAGE

This will probably represent a major portion of your baby shopping budget and, like the cot, contributes considerably to the look of the nursery. Although there are a few good quality bargains out there, generally with nursery furniture you get what you pay for.

Do you really need it?

You will need somewhere to store your baby's things although it need not be specific nursery furniture – any wardrobe and drawers will do.

When do you need it?

It can be useful to have the furniture set up before the birth so all your baby's kit is organised ready for their arrival. If this isn't possible it really won't be the end of the world if you sort it out after the birth. Consider that some furniture will have a long lead time – up to three months – so if you do want to get everything sorted before the big day, start shopping when you're around six months pregnant.

What will you need?

- **Plenty of storage space:** baby things are small but numerous and as babies grow, so does the amount of stuff they acquire. **Drawers** are essential, either within a changing unit (see page 97) or separately. They're useful not only for stowing clothes but for nappies, wipes, muslins, toiletries and general baby kit. A **wardrobe** is useful but not essential initially. Baby and toddler clothes are tiddly, so if you do get one, you could double hanging space by adding a second rail.

  A **changing unit** – again, these aren't vital but can be the saviour of a bad back if changing nappies on a mat on the floor is a strain. A unit also helps keep changing kit tidy and close-to-hand. Some parents use theirs throughout the nappy years, others abandon it and use the floor once their baby gets mobile amid worries of them rolling off. Cot-top changers save space in the more compact and bijou nursery, although they're a pain to lift on and off the cot.

  Some units are open-shelved, others have drawers and/or cupboards underneath. The latter cost more but have greater longevity, acting as storage beyond the nappy changing phase. Avoid the 'bath dresser' variety with an integral bath – they're a pain to fill with water, ugly and your baby will graduate to the main bath before long anyway. Worth considering is Ikea's great value open changing unit for under £20 – it isn't the sturdiest but will do the job.

TIP: if nursery space is at a premium, some furniture ranges offer under-cot drawers for extra storage.

Look for:

- Something that's *well-built* and can withstand the bashings of a boisterous toddler. Solid wood is more expensive than veneer but will last better. Solid MDF is a durable choice too.
- *Longevity* – furniture needn't be baby sized: your child will need help getting dressed for the foreseeable future anyway, so don't worry about whether they'll be able to reach into their cupboards when aged two or three. You can always add an extra, lower hanging rail to a full-sized wardrobe.
- Drawers with *built-in stoppers* to prevent older babies and toddlers dragging them out of the unit and dropping them.

Note also, that when choosing nursery furniture anything that looks cute for a baby might seem out of place in an older child's room. Somehow this is especially so for boys' bedrooms – older girls are less likely to mind those sweet cut-out hearts.

Kidsmill, Boori, King Parrot, Lemberk, Stokke, East Coast, The Children's Furniture Company, Ikea.

NURSERY/NURSING CHAIRS

Purpose-designed nursing chairs can be expensive and few would grace the pages of a stylish interiors mag but as a place to feed in comfort they're hard to better. They also provide a cosy bedtime story spot for many years.

You can of course feed your baby in bed or in a normal armchair, especially if you use a V-shaped pillow for back support. Additionally, if the chair is in the nursery and your baby is sleeping in your room for the first months, it might not be that appealing to switch rooms given you could just do the feed in bed.

If investing in one does appeal, Dutailier are the Rolls-Royce of nursery chairs. They're pricey (£250 plus), have old-fashioned looks (they wouldn't look out of place in a retirement home) but boy are they comfortable. Dutailiers glide, providing soothing movement for your baby. You can add a matching footstool (subject to space in the nursery – you could use a small table as a makeshift alternative). Note that if you want to improve the style a bit, you can get one made up with your own fabric via some nursery retailers.

A more stylish alternative to the Dutailiers is the Kensington Breastfeeding Chair designed by Dr Lynn Jones. This doesn't glide or rock but it does have an inflatable lumbar back support, is ergonomically designed for breastfeeding and has no sides so you can wrap a feeding cushion (see page 55–56) around you more easily to support your baby.

DECORATIONS

Some parents-to-be revel in creating a fully themed and co-ordinated nursery. Others take the view that for the first year or two their baby won't care if the walls are plain or the 'wrong' colour. Let's face it, baby girls with blue walls in their nursery aren't likely to be psychologically damaged by the experience.

An effective middle ground is to use a neutral paint on walls, adding pictures or wall stickers and accessories to create a theme. This will cost less and can be changed more easily once your no-longer-so-little-one finds wall-to-ceiling Winnie the Pooh a tad embarrassing when school mates come over.

Some decoration tips:

- If you're repainting, choose wipe-able, durable paint – toddlers don't respect paintwork.
- Think about longevity when choosing designs and patterns – avoid anything too babyish.
- Wall stickers (also known as 'decals') are a cheap and easy way to add a theme. Look for self-adhesive ones that can be removed easily. Try **www.wallglamour.co.uk**, **www.walliescutouts.co.uk**, Wall Candy, Next and Homebase.
- If you're repainting the nursery, do it well before your baby will spend time in there to limit exposure to paint fumes.

BLINDS AND CURTAINS

Blackout curtains or blinds help many babies to sleep better when it's light outside and will be worth every penny if they mean you get to sleep later in summer because the nursery remains dark. You can buy separate blackout linings to add to existing curtains if you aren't buying new ones. Generally we find blinds more effective than curtains as the latter still allow a little light through at the top and bottom.

If your child is susceptible to waking from the early morning sun, you can also buy a portable blackout blind called the 'Baa Baa Blind', which suctions onto any window up to a certain size and can be helpful when travelling.

TIP: fit a dimmer switch to the nursery so that you can keep lights low at bed time or during night feeds. If your baby becomes afraid of the dark as they get older, the Moonlight is an excellent low-energy night light which costs under a pound a year to run, even if it's on all the time.

OTHER ACCESSORIES

If you want to go the whole hog with everything from co-ordinating nappy tidies to frilly aprons and canopies for the cot, that's your call, but of course these are finishing touches rather than essentials and few of these items will be in use for very long.

7

Sleeping – bedding

Shopping list

✓ Bedding (if using a smaller first bed you will need two sets in different sizes):

- 3 or 4 fitted sheets
- 2 mattress protectors
- 2 or 3 sleeping bags OR 4 blankets and 3 or 4 flat top sheets

? Swaddling wrap

? Cot separator (for twins only)

? Sleep positioners

? Baby sheepskin

? Cat net (essential if you have a cat)

? Cot bumpers

? Coverlets

✗ Pillows and quilts (not for babies under 12 months)

Bedding is one of the most jargon-free and relatively simple aspects of baby shopping. We haven't yet seen boasts of 'anti-colic systems' or 'high tech breathability technology' when it comes to sheets or blankets – although the way the baby industry is going these could be just around the corner.

The main decision you'll face is whether to go with the traditional 'sheets and blanket' combination or the increasingly popular sleeping bags when tucking your little one up at bedtime (or not, in the case of the latter, as no tucking in is required).

The fabulous baby sleeping bag

Baby sleeping bags might appear to the uninitiated like another new-fangled way to ensure you part with yet more cash when baby shopping but as far as we're concerned, they're one of the baby industry's best inventions.

They're worn like little coats that zip down the front or popper at the shoulders but are closed at the bottom and usually sleeveless to help prevent overheating. Note the bags must be the right size for your baby so their head can't slip down through the neck hole. Normal night-clothes are worn underneath, according to the weight of the bag and the temperature in the nursery.

The bags are usually made from either T-shirt type jersey, light tow-elling or woven cotton. Organic versions are now also available. Most winter-weight bags have a polyester filling but some are 100% cotton.

There are plenty of baby product options where the answer to the question 'which is best?' is 'it depends' but this isn't one of them. As far as we're concerned (and our parent panel), there's no debate – sleeping bags beat conventional baby bedding hands down.

The only exception is during the first few weeks when some newborns benefit from swaddling (being wrapped snugly in a sheet, light blanket or special swaddling blanket – see page 112).

Why do we like sleeping bags so much? Well, it's all ultimately about maximising you and your baby's chances of getting a decent night's sleep – need we say more?

The main benefits are:

- Unlike blankets they can't get kicked off in the night – even young babies wriggle around and knock their covers off, exposing their little limbs to the cold and causing unnecessary waking.
- They mean less worrying about how much bedding the baby needs or what they should wear to bed. Bags come with tog ratings (see page 106) to give an indication of warmth, whereas blankets are of varying thicknesses and materials so temperature guidelines saying 'use two blankets if the nursery is x degrees' can be misleading.
- They help stop adventurous toddlers climbing out of the cot (potentially injuring themselves), thereby delaying the move to a proper bed.
- When travelling, they take up less space in luggage and are familiar even if the cot and room your baby sleeps in are not.
- Your baby remains nice and warm during night feeds because they can stay in their bag (although some can be fiddly for night time nappy changes).
- Perhaps most importantly of all, there's no worrying about blankets ending up over your baby's head.

Those on a tighter budget are sometimes put off sleeping bags as they're perceived as more expensive than blankets – they used to cost at least £20 to £25 each and you need two or three sizes to cover the baby and toddler years. However, recently supermarkets like Asda and Tesco and discount retailers have been offering them for as little as £10 each (although sometimes these don't display a tog rating). Most parents who've tried them think sleeping bags are well worth any extra money compared to blankets and we firmly agree.

Do you really need them?

Yes, unless for some reason you'd prefer conventional bedding.

When do you need them?

Although you can use some sleeping bags from birth, most are not suitable for babies under 10lbs and there's an argument that for very new babies blankets and sheets are better for a few weeks as they allow you to swaddle and provide more flexibility to add and remove layers.

Our suggestion is that if your baby will initially sleep in a Moses basket, carrycot, crib or hammock, start off with pram-sized sheets and blankets and switch to sleeping bags after a month or two. The blankets you buy won't be wasted as you can still use them on the pram. If you plan to introduce sleeping bags at some stage, it makes sense to do so before your baby moves to a proper cot, to avoid buying a full set of cot-sized blankets and top sheets too.

If you'd prefer to use sleeping bags from day one, it's safe to do so if you ensure the bag is the right weight for the room temperature and the correct size. We've found that some bags labelled 0-12 months are really better suited to babies from three months, so choose a newborn one and check it against your baby to make doubly sure (crucially the neck hole mustn't be so big your baby's head could slip down into the bag). The best-known brand, Grobag (rather like Hoovers are to vacuuming, 'Grobag' is sometimes used generically by parents as a synonym for sleeping bags), has a range for babies weighing as little as 6lbs.

Tog ratings

Most baby sleeping bags are labelled with a tog rating indicating the warmth they provide. These can seem surprisingly low – whilst an adult duvet might be 10 or 13 tog, baby sleeping bags are usually either 1 or 2.5 tog. Don't worry, junior won't be shivering away – 2.5 tog is perfectly adequate for a baby even for winter, and you can always add an extra layer of nightclothes underneath.

Choose bags according to the seasons that the size you are buying will cover:

- For spring, summer and autumn 1 tog – these also work well year round for daytime naps if your baby is fully dressed.
- For winter, we recommend 2.5 togs unless you tend to keep the nursery quite warm, in which case 1 tog should suffice.

Summer-weight 0.5 tog bags are also available and are great for very warm weather, holidays or visits to the grandparents if, like ours, they insist on keeping the house heated to tropical temperatures at all times.

How many?

Buy at least two sleeping bags, three if you can afford it (one on, one in the wash and a spare clean in case of accidents).

Look for:

Essential:

- *No sleeves or hood* – sleeves are not necessary for a baby sleeping bag. Only buy one with sleeves if they can be removed to prevent over-heating. Hoods are a complete no-no as babies' heads should be uncovered in bed.

- A bag that's *washable* at 40° or more and can go in the tumble dryer.

- A *secure fastening* – some zip down the front, others have poppers on the shoulders and a zip around the edge. Newborns need their nappies changing in the night, so check you'll be able to undo the bottom of the bag only, rather than having to take the whole thing off. For older babies the bag should be 'escape proof' with the zip ending at the bottom rather than the top. Some have two zips for extra security – you can also put the bag on the wrong way round to make the zip harder for an older baby to undo. Check zips and fastenings won't irritate your baby if, when they are older, they choose to sleep on their tummy.

Useful:

- A bag that's *tog rated* so you have a better idea of the warmth it will provide and the clothes needed underneath.

- *Car seat harness compatibility* – if you think you will travel by car a lot after bedtime these allow you to transfer your baby to and from the car and cot with less disturbance.

What bedding do babies need according to the room's temperature?

Room temperature:	Traditional bedding:	Sleeping bag tog rating:
75degrees F, 24°C	Sheet only	0.5 tog
70degrees F, 21°C	Sheet + one layer of blankets	1 tog
65degrees F, 18°C	Sheet + two layers of blankets	2.5 tog
60degrees F, 16°C	Sheet + three layers of blankets	2.5 tog plus one layer of blankets

Note: one blanket folded in two is equivalent to two layers of blankets

Many retailers now stock organic baby bedding made from cotton or bamboo that was grown without pesticides or chemical treatments. As a bonus, organic products are usually softer next to delicate newborn skin, although they do cost a bit more.

★ *Grobag.*

BLANKETS

There are some gorgeous baby blankets on the market but these are a popular gift for newborns so don't be tempted to buy too many. Baby blankets need to be one thing more than anything else – washable. Don't even think of buying one that is dry clean or hand wash only no matter how beautiful it is.

Baby blankets tend to come in one of four fabrics:

1. *Cellular cotton:* loosely woven so there are 'holes' in the blanket. Traditionally the most popular material for baby blankets. The loose weave means they're cool in summer and warm in winter – although if the holes are too big, little fingers and toes can get stuck. They're light and breathable to help prevent overheating and good for layering.
2. *Cellular acrylic:* warmer than cotton-cellular but not as gentle for sensitive skin. Sometimes a cotton/acrylic mix is used.
3. *Fleece:* usually too warm for the nursery but ideal on the pram if it's very cold. Super soft, easy to wash and quick drying.
4. *Wool:* also nice and warm so useful for the pram on cold days but ensure they're machine washable as not all wool is.

Note that babies under 12 months of age shouldn't sleep with pillows or quilts.

Do you really need them?

You will need a few small blankets for the pram even if you'll use sleeping bags at bedtime.

When do you need them?

From birth.

How many?

- Three lighterweight blankets in Moses basket/crib size (only two if you are going to use sleeping bags from birth)
- Two wool or fleecy pram blankets (only one if you buy a cosytoe/footmuff – see page 134) for very cold days. Any lighter blankets you use in a Moses basket or crib can also be used on the pram/pushchair in slightly warmer weather.
- Three or four in cot/cot-bed size (only one if you're using sleeping bags – it will be useful as a back-up extra layer if it's exceptionally cold).

We don't recommend buying any small receiving blankets, as we think shaped swaddling wraps are easier to use when wrapping up newborns (see page 112).

SHEETS

The main buying decisions:

1 Fitted or flat?

Fitted sheets make better bottom or undersheets than flat. They're less likely to wrinkle or come away from the mattress when your baby moves around and making the bed with them is easier. If you aren't going to use sleeping bags, you'll also need flat top sheets to layer with blankets.

Check the size of fitted sheets needed for your cot or cot-bed as mattress dimensions vary.

2 Which fabric?

Sheets for babies are either flat or fitted and are available in the following fabrics:

- woven cotton (cool for summer)
- flannelette: brushed cotton (warm in winter)
- terry: thin cotton or 'cotton mix' towelling which is usually stretchy
- cotton jersey: stretchy T-shirt-type material (fitted sheets only)

For fitted bottom sheets, we recommend cotton jersey. Their stretchiness makes bed-making easy and they fit snugly even if your mattress is an unusual size.

If you're buying top sheets for a Moses basket, crib or carrycot which will only be used for a few months, flannelette is a good choice for a winter newborn and woven cotton for a summer baby.

Top sheets for a cot or cot-bed will be used in all seasons, so woven cotton is probably your best bet, although remember these aren't necessary if you use sleeping bags.

When do you need them?

You'll need sheets for your baby's initial bed ready for the birth. If you aren't using a cot from birth, sheets for that can be bought later on.

How many?

- three to four fitted sheets, and an optional three to four flat (unnecessary if using shaped swaddling blankets, see page 112, or sleeping bags from birth) for the Moses basket, carrycot or crib in 'pram or crib size'. The latter are readily available in nursery shops but not usually found in general bedding stores. Obviously these won't be necessary if your baby sleeps in a cot from day one.

- three to four fitted sheets in cot/cot-bed size, and if you aren't using sleeping bags, three to four flat ones too.

Our recommended quantities are based on the idea of one on, one in the wash, one ready to go and, if you choose, one more spare.

★ *Zorbit, DK, Green Baby.*

TIP: if you'll use both a Moses basket and a carrycot buy pram size sheets for both rather than Moses basket ones. The pram sheets might be a little baggy on the Moses basket but when it comes to laundry you'll appreciate not having to sort out which is which when the size difference is so minimal.

MATTRESS PROTECTORS

If your chosen mattress doesn't have a waterproof cover, it's essential to add one as soggy bedding is inevitable at some stage with babies and clearing up will be a lot easier if nothing unpleasant has soaked through to the mattress. A breathable waterproof under-sheet is best. Waterproofing will stop the mattress getting wet or stained and breathability will help prevent overheating and clamminess.

Not all waterproof covers are the 'crinkly' variety; modern brushed cotton ones don't feel plasticky at all, as their waterproof layer of polyurethane is encased in two layers of cotton.

If you buy flat rather than fitted protectors, they can also be used during potty training and any bouts of vomiting over the top of your baby's normal sheets. Likewise pram-sized flat protectors for a carrycot, crib or Moses basket can double as portable changing mats and protection for car seats and buggies during potty training.

How many?

Two in pram/crib size and two in cot/cot-bed size.

★ *Hippychick.*

SWADDLING WRAPS/BLANKETS

Swaddling is a time-honoured way to calm new babies and help them feel more secure. Due to the Moro reflex, newborns often get startled by the unintentional movement of their own arms and legs. Swaddling keeps limbs tucked away and also exerts gentle pressure on the stomach to ease wind. It's something many parents swear by for their newborn (although a few babies don't like it).

Any thin blanket or large muslin can be used for swaddling but wrapping the blanket correctly can be frustratingly tricky, especially when a wriggly baby doesn't want to co-operate. Shaped swaddling blankets make it easier and are usually of an appropriate weight to avoid overheating. Choose a breathable, lightweight and washable fabric.

Swaddling blankets can provide an excellent stop-gap before introducing sleeping bags and we certainly recommend swaddling if your newborn is hard to settle.

How many?

Start off with one, see if your baby responds well to swaddling and, if so, buy a couple extra.

★ *Miracle Blanket, Grobag Swaddling Blanket.*

SHEEPSKINS

Research quoted in the likes of The Lancet has shown that sheepskin has a calming effect on newborns and regulates body temperature, being warm in winter but cool in summer. Sheepskins are even used in some hospital premature baby units – studies suggest their properties can help babies gain weight.

There have been worries about a link with cot death in the past but FSID's latest advice is that sleeping a baby on a sheepskin is OK as long as the baby sleeps on its back. Once they learn to roll onto their front, they should no longer sleep on the sheepskin. They can however still be used as a floor mat for sitting, playing or lounging on, rather than as a sleeping place.

Look for:

- A sheepskin *specifically for babies*
- One that is *washable* as cleaning baby vomit from a sheepskin's fibres with a cloth is a tough task. Special sheepskin shampoos are available for machine washing.

QUILTS AND COVERLETS

Quilts and duvets shouldn't be used as bedding before 12 months, by which time you might be happily using sleeping bags and reluctant to switch to a quilt anyway.

Coverlets are lighter in weight and most are labelled suitable for use from 7lb 7oz – around the average baby's birth weight. They're usually equivalent to a top sheet and fleece blanket but they offer less flexibility for adding or removing layers.

If you really must have the quilt that matches the rest of the nursery range you're buying, all is not lost as they can be used as floor mats for babies to sit or lie upon. Don't however be tempted to drape one over the side of the cot – it might look nice but could slip off onto a sleeping baby's head.

BUMPERS

These fabric-covered pads tie onto the bars of the cot or crib, making the sides softer if your baby ends up squashed against them. They also stop little limbs dangling out of the side of the cot and prevent soothers/dummies falling out. Finally, they sometimes allow parents to sneak out of the nursery unnoticed if your baby wants you around whilst they're dozing off – with a bumper in place, your early exit is less likely to be clocked.

Nearly all those sold in the UK are known as half bumpers and as the name suggests, only cover half of the cot. Full bumpers that go around the whole cot are common in the US but hard to find in Britain.

The problem with bumpers is that the window of time when they add to a baby's comfort is very short because once your little one starts pulling up, they must be removed so they can't be used by the more adventurous to climb out of the cot. For this reason, we think they're an optional rather than essential buy.

⚠ Check bumper ties regularly to ensure they are secure as long, loose ties could be hazardous. In the past there were concerns that bumpers could contribute to a baby overheating but recent research suggests they're neither good nor bad.

OTHER PRODUCTS FOR BEDTIME

Cat and mosquito nets

These fit over a baby's sleeping place to stop cats and nasty mozzies getting to your little one while they sleep.

Cat nets are stronger and quite rigid, whereas mosquito ones are typically made of lighter, finer weave material. Even if you think your darling puddy cat wouldn't hurt a flea, do get a cat net as there have been rare cases where cats have climbed into a cot, snuggled up next to the baby for a cuddle and sadly, the baby has suffocated.

Note that cat nets must be taut across the top of the cot or other baby sleeping place, as otherwise the net could collapse if the cat climbs on top of it.

Sleep positioners

Look through some of the specialist baby catalogues and you'll come across assorted baby 'sleep positioners'.

There are three main types:

1. *Those designed to keep babies on their backs* by preventing rolling over.
   These are unnecessary and aren't recommended by FSID. If babies are put to sleep on their backs from birth they'll be used to that position and, once they're old enough to roll over, are strong enough to sleep on their tummy or side.

2. *Those designed to keep babies on their sides* to prevent flat head syndrome (plagiocephaly).
   We aren't keen on these either. Flat head syndrome is where a baby develops a flat patch on the back of its head but it doesn't normally

cause discomfort and usually rights itself. The safest sleeping position for a newborn is on its back and the only exception is where a baby has specific health issues and a doctor advises you that they should sleep on their side or stomach. If this is the case, ask your doctor about the best way of achieving that. You can help prevent flat spots by encouraging plenty of 'tummy time' when your baby is out of the cot.

2 *Wedge-shaped positioners* designed to elevate a baby's head and shoulders – usually a foam wedge that sits on top of the mattress. These can be effective at reducing reflux and easing congestion if a baby has a cold. Try putting something sturdy like a couple of hardback books under the cot to raise the head end before buying one of these – this might work just as well. If you do buy one, it should be very firm to avoid any risk of suffocation.

Cot separators or dividers

These are small firm bolsters that fit horizontally across the cot between the side rails, separating the mattress into two sections. They're extendable to suit different cot widths.

They're usually marketed as a safety aid to keep your baby in the recommended 'feet to foot position', in which the baby's feet are at the foot of the cot with bedding reaching no higher than their armpits so they can't wriggle down under it. The idea of the divider is that it creates a false bottom if you want to sleep your baby at the top of the cot. In our opinion (and, more importantly, FSID's), these are unnecessary. Why are we so damning of them? Well firstly, if you use sleeping bags there's no need to keep a baby in the feet to foot position as there are no blankets to wriggle under anyway, and secondly even if you do use blankets, tucking your baby in well in the feet to foot position is easy to do and sufficient precaution.

The only exception to this is for twins – if you want them to start off sleeping in the same cot but in a space of their own, a divider can be useful.

8

Walking – pushchairs, slings and carriers

Shopping list

- ✓ Pram/buggy with a lie-flat seat or carrycot (unless using a sling/carrier all the time)
- ✓ Raincover
- ? Footmuff
- ? Sunshade and insect net
- ? Buggy weights
- ? Sling/carrier
- ✗ Pram parasol

PUSHCHAIRS

When we asked our parent panel which purchase for their baby they agonised over most, the pushchair was right at the top of the list. But why is selecting your baby's first wheels such a headache? It's probably due to a combination of too much choice, pushchairs having become something of a fashion statement, and the fact that the perfect pushchair doesn't exist, so looking for it is futile.

All these reasons combined mean some parents acquire a whole fleet of the things. The ownership record amongst our friends is five at once. Other people become serial buyers – buying one, flogging it second-hand, moving on to the next one – an expensive habit.

The advent of the 'must-have pram'

Pram purchases have become much more style–led recently. If pushing a chic-looking buggy or the celeb mums' current favourite appeals to you, that's fine but don't be seduced solely by style – check for practicality too. Conversely don't dismiss a stylish pram, assuming that because it looks flashy, it won't perform well – some of our favourites do well on both counts.

Pushchair terminology

Pram – although used generically for all types of baby wheels, strictly speaking this refers to a model with a carrycot.

Buggy – a lightweight pushchair with a semi-upright or upright seat (it might recline).

Travel system – a pushchair that accommodates an infant car seat. A model with 'travel system' as part of the name usually comes with a compatible car seat included (be sure to check it fits your vehicle before buying). Many other pushchairs can be turned into a travel system with the addition of a compatible car seat.

Two-in-ones/three-in-ones – a chassis plus either a carrycot and two-way facing pushchair seat ('three-in-one') for use later on, or a seat that reclines into a pram-style unit for a newborn but sits upright and faces both ways for older babies (a 'two-in-one').

Umbrella-folding buggy – a lightweight, compact buggy which folds long and narrow like an umbrella.

Telescopic-folding buggy – these fold shorter and wider than umbrella buggies and are often better than umbrella-folders for smaller car boots.

Consider that newborns should ideally lie flat ...

The optimal position for newborns is lying fully-flat at 180 degrees. This is better for spine development and breathing but not all newborn pushchairs offer this.

Fundamentally, you have three options for a newborn (some models offer more than one of these):

1. *A carrycot which attaches to a chassis*
   A carrycot is undoubtedly the best way to allow newborn babies to lie properly flat and should ideally be your starting point. Although a carrycot pram will only suit your baby for the first four to six months and might be expensive, most convert to buggies later on (sometimes referred to as three-in-ones) and a detachable carrycot can double as an overnight sleeping place, meaning you can skip buying a crib or Moses basket (provided the mattress is suitable – see pages 91–96).

2. *A forward facing or two in one pushchair that's 'suitable from birth'*
   Some pushchairs recline sufficiently to be labelled 'suitable from birth' under British Standards. Note this doesn't necessarily mean they lie fully-flat. Interestingly, UK standards are less stringent than elsewhere in Europe and a seat that's only acceptable from three months in France passes as 'suitable from birth' in the UK.
   For the health reasons mentioned already, we advocate that only

seats that lie fully-flat or very nearly so are really suitable for newborns for anything beyond very short periods.

Additionally, buggy seats can be flimsy and not as padded or supportive as a carrycot (though adding a sheepskin buggy liner might help). If a 'suitable from birth' pushchair is your only option for practical reasons, check how far the seat reclines and go for the one that lies flattest.

3 *A travel system with an infant car seat that attaches to the pushchair chassis (usually using adaptors) or clips onto the pushchair seat*

Nowadays many parents prioritise being able to whisk the car seat straight onto the pram, the idea being it avoids waking their baby who has fallen asleep in the car. However, the upright position of an infant carrier is not ideal for a baby's spinal and respiratory development. Whilst an upright seat protects a baby involved in a car accident better than a lie-flat one, out of the car, lying flat is preferable. And in reality, most newborns fall back to sleep quickly on the pushchair anyway even if transferred from car seat to pushchair.

If the ability to place the car seat straight onto the pushchair is something you really want or you regularly take taxis (see page 127), then go for an infant carrier that sits upright in a car but lies flat on the chassis. (See page 154 for more lie-flat car seats and compatible pushchairs).

Travel system packages all too often involve compromising because either the pushchair isn't the best choice for you or the car seat sold with it isn't (not all car seats fit all cars).

... but think longer term too

A common pitfall of this pushchair palaver is focusing overly on the newborn phase, rather than considering longer term needs too. Too many parents invest in a bulky and expensive contraption that's lovely and secure for their newborn, but gets traded in for a more practical, lightweight buggy once junior hits six months. The result – that costly first set of wheels gets sent to the pushchair graveyard and if it cost £300, that works out at an alarming £50 a month. If you'd prefer one pushchair to last through to toddlerhood, think of both the newborn and toddler stages. Later on you'll probably want a seat with some recline (it needn't be fully-flat) and a light, manoeuvrable buggy that folds easily.

One idea is to start with the upfront intention of buying two pushchairs – starting with something not too expensive, with a comfy lie-flat carrycot for the first months, and trading it for a smaller, lighter-weight option once your baby reaches six months. This means there's no need to compromise at either stage and can sometimes work out cheaper overall if you choose carefully.

When to buy

Whilst you won't need a pram the day your baby is born, soon after you'll probably want to head out for some fresh air. It makes sense to order it before the birth because if your preferred choice is out of stock you might have to wait up to eight weeks for delivery. It's a good idea to assemble the pram (if needed) and familiarise yourself with it before your new arrival turns up and turns your life upside down.

Take a test-drive

Many retailers let you test-drive pushchairs around the store and sometimes outside. Take a few for a spin to check how particular models 'handle'. Also, fold them up, put the carrycot/car seat on and off the chassis and test out key features.

Undoubtedly it's wise to invest time in choosing a buggy – this is one of the most expensive baby purchases you'll make and one of the easiest to mess up. But don't become obsessed with the pursuit of the perfect pram – no pram can possibly tick every box, so prioritise those features that matter to you most and be prepared to sacrifice some of the minor ones.

££ Money-saving tips for pushchair-purchasers

- Buy 'nearly new' – some people's serial pram-buying habits provide rich pickings for anyone after barely used second-hand models.
- Check out last season's ranges (most manufacturers change fabrics and colours once or twice a year). You might find old models at a discount. A savvy shop assistant will know when new ranges launch and when old models get marked down.
- Look after your pushchair with a view to selling it once you've finished with it. There's a healthy market for second-hand prams, so head to parenting websites' for sale sections, NCT 'nearly new sales', eBay or car boot sales.
- Don't feel pressured to buy the equivalent of a Ferrari if a Ford will do.

TIP: be wary of buying a very newly launched pram – many have teething troubles at first so it's better to stick with something tried and tested.

How to decide

When choosing a buggy it's crucial to think about your lifestyle. If several factors are important to you, you might need to compromise or invest in two prams for different situations (perhaps one or both could be bought second-hand to save money).

Be honest with yourself – an all-terrain pram for cross-country walks with your baby might appeal, but it will be far from ideal if your hiking expeditions usually involve strolling to Starbucks to grab a latte.

Consider:

1 Your home

If you live in an **upstairs** flat and can't leave a pram in the lobby, your best bet is a lightweight, easy-fold model. We hate to say it but even this won't be easy, as you'll have to fold it and carry it, plus baby, upstairs, along with any bags.

If you only have a couple of steps to scale, something sturdy with big wheels and decent suspension can be bumped carefully up and down with your baby in it.

If your home lacks **storage space**, a compact two-in-one buggy that's freestanding when folded is probably your best bet.

For staircases or lack of storage space – Maclaren Techno XT or XLR (both recline almost flat). Red Castle City Link (has a carrycot option), Micralite Toro or Fastfold (optional carrycot, one-handed fold in buggy mode, freestanding when folded). For those with just a few steps, Bugaboos, Micralites, Stokke Xplory (it has a two wheel 'stairs mode').

2 Where you'll go

Rough ground: if you'll frequently push the buggy along bumpy pathways, cross-country or on the beach, an all-terrain pushchair will be a must rather than the fashion accessory they have become. Decent suspension and large pneumatic wheels make pushing over rough ground easier. Some all-terrain prams now have foam-filled wheels which offer the best of both worlds – a smooth ride without the potential punctures of pneumatic tyres.

Even with an all-terrain pram, walking across very uneven ground should be avoided with young babies as their muscles cannot cope well with the jolting. A supportive sling or carrier is a better way to transport a newborn in such scenarios.

Mountain Buggy Urban and Terrain, Phil&Teds Sport and Vibe, Bugaboo Cameleon, Micralites with the optional 'all-terrain kit'.

Urban dwellers: good manoeuvrability and swivel (rather than fixed) wheels will be crucial. Wider prams can be a pain to get through shop doorways and aisles. Fixed wheel three-wheelers can be especially problematic around towns but plenty of pushchairs are well-suited to cities so you'll have a wide choice.

Bugaboo Cameleon or Bee, Quinny Zapp (one of the 'swivelliest', easiest-to-push buggies but only suitable from six months), Pliko Pramette, Silver Cross 3d, Bebe Confort Loola, Chicco Trio, any Maclaren.

3 How you'll travel

If you walk a lot, you might prefer a reversible seat unit so your baby can face you or look outwards. Research suggests having a baby facing their carer in the pushchair helps language development and bonding.

A generous shopping basket will be useful if you regularly shop on foot. Larger prams tend to have bigger baskets than lightweight buggies. Some models tip easily if you put heavy shopping on the handlebars but 'buggyweights' can help prevent this – see page 00.

For reversible seats: Bugaboos, Bebe Confort Loola, iCandy Cherry, Stokke Xplory. For larger shopping baskets: iCandy Cherry, Bugaboos (we know they keep coming up but their versatility means they deserve recommendation across categories).

Car users – check whether the pushchair fits in your **car boot** – measure up carefully. Ideally once it's in there, you should have space for other things too, especially for holidays or overnight trips.

Check the pushchair is **easy to lift** – getting a heavy pram in and out of your boot can literally be a pain, especially if you've had a c-section. It's not just a question of comparing weights on paper – one 8kg pram can feel a lot heavier than another depending on the way it folds and, consequently, the way you have to lift it.

Finally, think about **how easily it folds and unfolds** as you'll do this frequently if you use the car a lot. Some prams fold in one piece, others only once you remove the seat unit or carrycot. 'Two-piecers' are fiddlier but the weight is split so each piece is lighter. Avoid very heavy, bulky models – they can be annoying to get into the boot and take up a lot of space.

For small boots: Graco Mosaic or Mirage, Bugaboo Bee or Cameleon (with its handle contracted down).

Bus and train users – many bus companies now allow passengers on without having to fold pushchairs but do check how things work on routes you'll use.

If you travel by bus or train a lot and need to collapse the pushchair, a one-hand-fold will be crucial. Try a few out as some supposedly one-hand-fold buggies definitely need two hands despite what the manufacturers say.

A better option for public transport might be to use a sling or carrier until your baby is old enough for a light one-hand-fold buggy such as a Micralite or Maclaren.

Micralite Fastfold (folds one-handed in buggy mode – although even this is not so easy to open again one-handed. Note: the newborn carrycot mode won't be easier than other options for public transport). If you really need a pushchair that's suitable from birth and folds easily, go for a Maclaren with a lie-flat seat. Less widely available is the Aprica Pram First, which has an easy one-hand-fold and a lie-flat, reversible seat.

We don't generally like travel systems for newborns but if you use **taxis** frequently, these will be your only reasonable option, allowing you to carry your own car seat with you. You can take the car seat off the chassis, secure the baby in the taxi and put the chassis in the boot or on the floor of a black cab.

Lie-flat car seats are particularly worthwhile for taxi-users as at least the baby can stay flat when the car seat is on the pram (although the upright position is safer when travelling in a moving vehicle – see page 154). You should also prioritise a model with a chassis that folds easily.

Jane Matrix (lie-flat car seat compatible with some Jane chassis), Mamas & Papas Pro Sleep car seat (compatible with any pushchair that takes the Maxi-Cosi Cabriofix car seat).

If you'll be **flying** a lot, choose something that folds easily, can tackle sand or rough ground (depending on your destinations) and is light. Many parents invest in a Maclaren or similar for holidays but small wheels make them a nightmare to push on beaches or uneven paths.

Quinny Zapp (for city holidays post- six months – see below), Micralite Fastfold (for beach/rural holidays from six months), Maclaren. (For city holidays, some models are suitable from birth.)

Product showcase – a superb choice for frequent travellers is the Quinny Zapp. It folds up to a tiny 69x27x30cm and weighs only 6kg. Smaller-wheeled pushchairs are not usually smooth to push but the Zapp's innovative design tackles this and it's very easy to steer even with an older, heavier child in it. The downsides – the seat unit isn't suited to newborns as it doesn't recline (although you can use a Maxi-Cosi infant car seat on it for short periods). It doesn't have a shopping basket and although supremely manoeuvrable, the small rubber wheels don't cope well with sand or uneven surfaces.

4 If you might have another baby soon

If you might end up with a second baby relatively soon after number one (by choice or otherwise), it's worth looking at pushchairs that start as singles and convert into tandem-style doubles – and back again, once your oldest is walking everywhere. These are highly flexible, although they are bigger and heavier than most standard single models.

The best known of these are made by Phil&Teds. Some parents worry that the second seat on these prams is too close to the ground but owners report this isn't a problem and many like the optional newborn cocoon (a soft carrycot).

Phil&Teds Sport (three-wheeler with a swivel front wheel) and Vibe models, or the iCandy Apple (called the 'Pear' in 'twin' mode – see page 129).

Product showcase – the iCandy Apple/Pear is fairly new to the market at the time of writing but offers unusual flexibility, not only converting from single to double (and back) but also allowing the choice of two carrycots, two car seats or two pushchair units. With two seat units or carrycots it is quite long. Even if you have children of different ages, both units always have to face the same direction, and the lower tier is out of view. However it is worth considering for siblings who are close in age.

5 If you're having twins

For twins, your first decision is between a 'tandem' (one child sits behind the other) and a 'side-by-side'.

A comparison of tandems and side-by-sides for twins:

	Tandems	Side-by-sides
Manoeuvrability	Can be very long, making crossing roads problematic. Getting through doorways/shop aisles is easier though	Width can make doorways and shop aisles tricky. Check any you consider will fit through standard doorways
Can the babies interact with each other?	Not easily (although this is good as well as bad as they can't steal each other's biscuits/toys)	Yes, once they can lean forward and peer round the seat divide
Do both seats recline?	Depends on the model	Yes on most models
Can they both see out?	Visibility will be limited for the rear child unless their seat is elevated	Both get a decent view

Overall, we prefer side-by-sides for twins, provided they fit through normal doorways – not all do, so check. If you do go for a tandem for twins, choose one where the rear seat is elevated enough for the second twin to see out. Also watch out for very long models which can make crossing roads perilous because the front of the pram will be so far ahead of you.

A few twin pushchairs have optional carrycots – either two singles or a double shared by both babies. Generally, single carrycots are easier to handle if you anticipate detaching the carrycot quite often. Look for pneumatic wheels which usually go hand in hand with decent suspension for twin prams as these make pushing two toddlers (which your newborns will eventually be) easier.

Jane PowerTwin (well-priced, both babies can see out, easy-to-push, light), Mountain Buggy Urban (pricey but durable, single and double carrycot options so both babies can lie-flat, facing you), Out n About Nipper Twin 360 (similar to the Mountain Buggy but cheaper, no carrycot but very lightweight and easy to push side-by-side). iCandy Pear (see page 129, quite flexible as it can take two carrycots or two car seats, but the line of vision is problematic and it's too new, at the time of writing, to know about any teething problems).

Twin tip: for family outings and holidays it might be worth investing in two cheap single buggies as well as your double pushchair. When you and your partner are together, you can take one pram each. If the buggies are the same type, you can buy pushchair connectors (Prince Lionheart do some) cheaply to fit them together for when one of you is alone with the babies.

6 If you want to jog with your baby

If jogging with your baby appeals, you'll need a lightweight fixed wheel three-wheeler. You should not jog with a baby under six months and, unless a fixed-wheel three wheeler would suit the rest of your lifestyle (if you live in the country), we suggest waiting until your baby reaches six months as you'll have more choice, including some cheaper models that are only suitable after that age.

Out n About Sport, Baby Jogger Performance, Mountain Buggy Terrain.

All-rounders

If no single issue stands out for you, our 'all-rounders' make solid choices – they're a great bet in most scenarios and should take you through the whole period from birth until your pram-pushing days are over.

For most people, something with a detachable carrycot, that later converts to a lightweight, easy-to-fold buggy will offer the best value and reduce the chance of you trading in your first pram later on.

Bugaboo Cameleon, Micralite Toro or Fastfold, Mamas & Papas Pliko Pramette (no detachable carrycot and smaller wheels than the others but OK for city streets and parks).

££ If you think you could manage solely with a sling or carrier for the first few months, you could skip the carrycot/lie-flat phase, and buy only a cheaper, lightweight buggy later on. A reclining seat will still be important if you want your baby to nap in the buggy but it needn't lie completely flat once your baby is older.

Look for:

For all types of prams, there are some generic features to look for.

Essential:

- An *adjustable or appropriate height handle* – especially if you/your partner/other regular carers are very different heights. This won't be a problem on most prams unless you are particularly short or tall.

- *Decent brakes* – look for brakes on two wheels not just one.
- *Good manoeuvrability* – a lighter-weight pram might be easier to lift in and out of the car than a heavy one but won't necessarily be easier to push. Swivel wheels that can also be fixed in position are beneficial because you can adjust them to suit different terrain. Suspension and wheel-type affect manoeuvrability too. Check whether you can push the buggy one-handed, which can be useful. Bar handles are good for this.
- A *comfortable-looking seat* and ideally one in a breathable fabric to prevent your baby getting clammy in hot weather. Adding a sheepskin liner can help with this though. The harness should be well-padded.
- A *smooth, easy-to-use recline* mechanism – some will jolt your baby awake when you are trying to recline the buggy or can be fiddly.
- *Foam-covered or soft plastic handles* are more comfortable than hard plastic.
- A model that's *light and easy to move when folded.*
- Something that's relatively *simple to fold.*
- An *adjustable, padded harness.*

Useful:

- A *reversible seat* allows your baby to face you, encouraging interaction, or to face out so they can see the world better – whichever you and they prefer.
- *Pneumatic or foam-filled wheels* make for a smoother ride for your baby and easier pushing for you. Pneumatic wheels can puncture and will need pumping up from time to time (lining the inner wheel with Slime sealant will help prevent punctures).
- *A generous basket* – useful for carrying the incredible amount of stuff

that you need for a baby. Oh, and you might just manage to fit some shopping in too. Check it is easily accessible even when the buggy seat is reclined.

Don't worry about:

- *Car seat compatibility* – as we've already said, sitting in a car seat for too long isn't good for your baby. Be careful as the one that comes with a particular travel system might not fit in your car or might not perform well in crash tests.
- Whether *accessories* such as raincovers, footmuffs, umbrellas and insect nets are included. Although this will contribute to the 'real' price of the pushchair, most extras can be bought separately and some are unnecessary anyway (see below).
- *Bumper bars* – some toddlers like holding onto these but they can get in the way when lifting your child in and out.
- The *size of the buggy's hood* – almost all integral sun canopies are fairly useless. Some larger hoods have clear 'viewing windows' which are useful but really not essential.

TIP: if you aren't shy, approaching people in the street who are pushing a pram you're considering and asking them if they're happy with it is a great way to get the lowdown.

TIP: be careful about buying a new-to-the-market pushchair – it's common for these to suffer from glitches that will be ironed out by the manufacturers later on but could cause problems in early versions.

PUSHCHAIR ACCESSORIES

Some pushchairs include co-ordinating accessories, others charge a small fortune for them. Generic alternatives are often cheaper and will perform as well, and sometimes better.

Sun protection

Carrycots come with a hood and apron which will offer good protection. All but the cheapest buggies have integral canopies/hoods but these aren't much use on their own. Parasols are also pretty ineffective unless you stay in a fixed spot – when you're walking the sun will be in different directions all the time.

A sun shade that fits over the whole buggy is much better and some pushchair manufacturers now offer these as part of their co-ordinated range.

Outlook Shade-a-babe (a universal UV shade).

Raincovers

Most buggies and carrycots come with raincovers. You can buy generic ones separately from nursery stores but these might not fit quite as well as the ones specifically designed for that pushchair

Footmuffs/cosytoes

These are like little outdoor sleeping bags for use on the pushchair. They aren't essential but help keep your baby cosy in colder weather. Unlike blankets, a footmuff cannot fall (or be kicked) off the buggy into a muddy puddle. Note, footmuffs aren't needed for carrycots as these provide better weather protection than buggies and you can use pram blankets without them falling off. Choose one with a zip-off front/top for easy removal and access to your baby. This type can double as buggy liners in summer.

Sheepskin-lined versions are more breathable than those with a synthetic lining and help regulate temperature.

Generic footmuffs can be bought from nursery stores and are often cheaper than branded ones from a particular pushchair range. It won't be the end of the world if it doesn't match the buggy fabric exactly but do check it will fit the seat and harness properly.

Sheepskin liners

These keep babies cooler in summer and warmer in winter, have properties that are believed to calm and soothe babies and are a great way to make a flimsy lightweight buggy seat more comfortable. However, their bulk can make it hard to fold umbrella buggies, so bear this in mind. Check for pre-cut holes for the buggy's harness to feed through and machine washability.

Travel bags

Generally travel bags are only worthwhile if you'll frequently travel by plane and have to stow the pushchair in the hold – they'll provide protection from wear and tear. Countless prams do get damaged in transit and so buying one can ultimately save you money and aggravation. Either wait and see if you need one depending on your travel plans or, if you have a friend with a similar-sized pushchair, see if you can share the cost of a travel bag if it is unlikely your holidays will clash.

Pram toys

These are a welcome way to keep babies occupied when shopping. Their advantage over ordinary toys is they clip on and therefore can't be dropped or lobbed off (there is truth in that old phrase 'throwing your toys out of the pram').

> *Tiny Love Take Along Arch, Buggybooks (clip-on board books for older babies), Baby Whoozit Spirals.*

Buggy weights

If your pram is tippy (and some are, especially if you hang shopping over the handles), you can add buggy weights to the front wheels to rebalance it. They're cheap and don't adversely affect manoeuvrability so are definitely worth investing in if you find your pram is vulnerable to this problem.

SLINGS AND CARRIERS

See page 199 for toddler back carriers.

Slings and carriers have a slightly hippy image in some people's eyes but we're huge fans and so are legions of other parents who've found that 'wearing' their baby is good for them and for their little one.

Baby wearing comes into its own on countless occasions, from the everyday – freeing hands for chores at home if your baby doesn't like being put down, 'buggy-free' shopping trips, or jumping on the bus without folding and dragging a pram on – to rarer occasions such as ambling across countryside that even the most rugged of all-terrain prams couldn't cope with, or at the airport if your buggy isn't returned to you at the plane steps. Most importantly of all, the majority of babies love being carried this way.

The terms 'slings 'and 'carriers' are used pretty interchangeably but strictly speaking, slings are less structured and more 'fabricy' whereas carriers have more buckles and straps and a padded 'seat' for the baby to sit in, usually in an upright position.

Reasons to love baby wearing

Benefits for babies:

- Being carried in a sling/carrier is comforting, like an extension of the womb. It promotes bonding and is especially positive for babies with colic or reflux.
- Babies view and interact with the world from a higher vantage point and are more 'included' in conversations than in prams.

Benefits for you:

- The closeness to your baby can be heart-warming (and literally body-warming – lovely when it's chilly although less so on a scorching day).
- If your baby is the type who screams when you put them down or needs rocking to sleep, you can keep hands free to tackle the million tasks involved in being a new parent.
- You can leave the pushchair behind.
- They're practical on occasions when a pram can be a liability, such as country walks, crowded places and on public transport. When shopping, you can skip the lift and get through aisles/doors/up escalators more easily than with a pram.
- Some slings/carriers allow for discreet breastfeeding – ideal if you feel shy about 'public exposure'.
- If you also have a toddler still needing a pushchair, you can put your newborn in a sling/carrier to bridge the gap until the older one can walk all the time or use a buggy board. This might allow you to avoid buying the dreaded double buggy which might only be needed for a few months.

Twin tip: Assuming there aren't always two adults around, there are still options when it comes to 'wearing' twins. You could use a single wrap or ring sling (see page 142) to hold two young babies or you could wear two slings, one for each baby. There are also a few specialist 'double' carriers about, such as The Weego (try **www.TwinsUK.co.uk**). Obviously carrying two babies at once will be more of a strain so you might not manage to do it for long.

If at first you don't succeed...

If we think slings/carriers are so indispensible, how come most of us know people who bought one, tried it and gave up? The problem is that the first few times you use them, the majority are Krypton-Factor-esque – possibly worse given no task on the Krypton Factor ever involved holding a wriggly, wobbly-headed newborn at the same time. Using a carrier takes practice and can be intimidating to get your baby in and out of initially, especially if you're worried about upsetting, or worse dropping, your baby whilst sorting out a tangle of buckles and straps.

So choose a model that's easy to use and persevere. If a friend has the same one, ask them to show you how to use it. If not, ask someone at the shop to do a demo or at least get someone else to help the first few times. If the instruction leaflet is confusing, check the internet for video demos. Practising with a doll might feel silly but could help. Your efforts will be rewarded, we promise.

So can I do without a pram then?

Whilst we know a couple of parents who've managed without a pram by carrying their children in slings, most people use theirs in addition to a pram. Certainly, if baby carrying really appeals, it's quite realistic to use only a sling/carrier for the first months, dodging the lie-flat pram stage. Once your baby gets too heavy to carry around so much, they'll be old enough for a lighter-weight, cheaper buggy.

Overall though, we recommend slings/carriers as a complement to a pram. Sometimes a pram is genuinely easier – for instance, eating and drinking with a baby in a front carrier can be tricky. You could try managing with just the carrier and seeing how you get on.

Where to buy?

Most nursery retailers carry only a limited range. For more choice, try online sling specialists such as Little Possums, Bigmamaslings or The Carrying Kind – these guys live and breathe slings/carriers and will work with you to find one to suit your needs. Some specialists offer hire services, so you can see if you get on with a particular brand before buying.

Another way to try before you buy is at a get-together organised by **slingmeet.co.uk** – check their website to find out when the next meeting near you is. You can also ask 'experienced' baby wearers questions on the site's forum.

Front or back? In or out?

In the beginning, you'll need to carry your baby on your front, usually facing in until they can support their own head, and then outwards later on.

Until what age you manage to carry your baby on your front before your back and shoulders hurt depends on which model you have, your own strength and stature and whether your baby is a bruiser or a tiddler. Typically we find mums can use a front carrier until their baby is around six months before stopping or switching to a back carrier (see page 199), while dads usually manage for a little longer. Sling types that distribute babies' weight well can give you up to 18 months of carrying in front and a few, mostly wrap slings and also the Ergo (see page 141), can be used on both front and back.

> ££ Slings and carriers lend themselves well to second-hand purchase. Most are washable so won't seem much different if they're 'pre-used'.

Types of slings/carrier:

1 Soft carriers

These 'structured' carriers (the best known is the BabyBjorn) hold the baby next to your chest in an upright position. They usually have a padded section for the baby to sit in and adjustable straps and buckles to position the carrier correctly. A padded flap provides support for a newborn's floppy head when they face inwards and this flap is then folded down when the baby moves to the forward-facing position once they can support their own head.

- ⊕ Can feel more secure than slings and for many people are easier to use.
- ⊕ Good for windy babies as there's slight pressure on the digestive system. Babies with reflux also benefit from the upright rather than more horizontal position of most slings.
- ⊕ Adjustable to fit different-sized wearers.
- ⊖ Fewer carrying positions than some slings.
- ⊖ Not as suited to breastfeeding as some slings.
- ⊖ There are concerns (although there's no firm evidence) that some carriers provide inadequate support in this upright position which

can result in too much pressure bearing down from the head onto the baby's spine.

- Some have a minimum weight of 8lbs or more – although this isn't an issue for long unless you have a small or premature baby.

Verdict: this is personal choice territory – some parents prefer the look of structured carriers and find slings too 'hippyish'. If you're unlikely to persevere with instructions, a carrier might suit you better than a sling.

Bushbaby Cocoon for longevity, BabyBjorn for ease of use, the Wilkinet or Ergo for weight distribution.

Product showcase – the Ergo is unusual amongst more structured carriers because it can be worn on either your front or back and therefore can be used from birth (with the optional newborn insert) right through the toddler years. Older babies and toddlers love the back carrying position, which is rather like a supported piggyback, and younger babies are in a more supportive, less upright position than with other carriers.

Product showcase – Another of our favourite products, The Wilkinet, is a cross between a carrier and a wrap sling (see below) with slightly more structure and plenty of padding for comfort. It's a great middle ground between a BabyBjorn type carrier and a standard wrap and has several carrying positions. Its only drawback is that you have to sit down to put it on, which isn't always practical.

Ergo and Wilkinet slings

2 Wrap slings

Fundamentally these are long pieces of fabric that wrap around wearer and baby, securing them in place. They offer the best longevity amongst slings because they're highly supportive for newborns and easy to breastfeed in and, unlike most pouches or ring slings, some offer a back carrying position for older babies/toddlers. They also distribute weight more evenly across your whole torso. But they can be quite daunting to use at first, so aren't ideal if you aren't the persevering type.

Some wraps are made from stretchy T-shirt type material, others from woven cotton. The former are lovely and cosseting but some stretch too much to support a heavier, older baby.

- ⊕ Several carrying positions – including on the back – mean some of these slings can be used until your baby is 18 to 24 months old.
- ⊕ They work well for carrying premature babies as they are so supportive.
- ⊕ One size usually fits all for stretchy wraps (woven wraps tend to come in different sizes).
- ⊕ Their upright carrying positions are great for babies with reflux or colic and the hammock positions well-suited to breastfeeding.
- ⊕ Easy to wash and dry, and pack reasonably small.
- ⊖ Tricky to master at first – you'll need to persevere.

Verdict: Our favourite type of sling – but steer clear if you give up easily on things. Amongst traditional wraps we prefer stretchy fabric to woven, although they might not work for quite so long with heavy toddlers.

★ *Hug-a-bub*

3 Ring slings

A length of fabric that threads through two attached rings, allowing easy adjustment. Some have a padded section to provide extra comfort for the baby – especially nice for a newborn – but this can limit how adjustable the sling will be, which can be a problem if you and your partner are very different in size. Padding also means the sling will take up more space in your bag (although they're still very compact) and could be too warm in mid-summer.

Similar in design to standard ring slings but with an easy-adjust buckle rather than rings are the likes of the Premaxx 'baby bag' and Baba Sling. The Baba Sling has a padded shoulder which stops the fabric digging into you and aids comfort.

- ⊕ Adjustability means both partners can use the same sling.
- ⊕ Well-suited to breastfeeding in.
- ⊕ Non-padded ring slings pack small.
- ⊖ Can take some getting used to at first (although after the initial period they are easy to use).
- ⊖ Not ideal for an older baby if you have a bad back.

Verdict: we aren't big fans of the standard ring slings but some people swear by them. Slings that are padded only in the shoulder, like the Maya, are a good compromise between comfort and adjustability.

Maya, PreMaxx, Baba Sling.

4 Pouch slings

These are a simple tube or sash of fabric worn over one shoulder – not dissimilar to a sling for broken arms. They're very easy to use with no confusing buckles or straps: you just put the baby in the little pouch of fabric and go. They're a good choice if you'll take the baby in and out a lot. The big downside is that these slings come in quite specific sizes and the wrong size will not be comfortable for you, secure for the baby or fit different-sized wearers.

- ⊕ Very easy to use.
- ⊕ Compact – can be shoved in a bag.

- ⊕ Hold newborns in a 'natural' reclined position, akin to cradling a baby in your arms.
- ⊕ Several different carrying positions so work well for newborns and toddlers alike (the latter only for short periods though).
- ⊖ Not adjustable.
- ⊖ Weight is concentrated on one shoulder (with the exception of the Tricotti), so not distributed evenly – a problem for longer use with heavier babies and toddlers.

> **Product showcase** – unlike most pouches the Tricotti has two pieces of fabric rather than one, so it goes over both shoulders. This distributes weight much more evenly and means it can be used for older babies and toddlers. It's also hugely practical as it packs away so small. The Tricotti won't fit very petite or large wearers though and you'll need to be careful to buy the right size.
>
> *Tricotti sling*

Verdict: if a pouch appeals, the Tricotti is hard to beat.

The Tricotti, amongst more traditional pouches: the Hotslings and Brightsparks Coorie.

Look for:

Whichever type of sling or carrier appeals, here are some features to consider.

Essential:

- *Ease of use* – if not, you'll be less likely to use it.
- *'Washability'* – most but not all are machine washable.
- *Comfort and security for your baby* – a good sling will be comfortable for your baby and supportive, so you can move around without feeling the need to keep a hand on your baby.

- *Comfort for you* – especially if you want to continue to use a carrier/sling as your baby gets heavier, or if you have a bad back, choose something that distributes weight evenly. Anything that concentrates weight on your upper back and shoulders, or is one-sided, will be hard to use once a baby is heavier. Look for wide straps in carriers and adjustability.

Useful:

- *Longevity* – if you want to use one sling/carrier through to the toddler years, look at the recommended *weight range* and choose one with *several different carrying positions* – newborns are best carried on your front facing in, older babies and toddlers will want to face outwards so they have something to look at. Models that carry a toddler on your hip or back are better for later on.
- *Unisex* fabric and fit – if both you and your partner will use the sling, you might want to avoid anything flowery or girly. Most slings/carriers adjust to fit a range of builds but a few, especially pouch slings, come in specific sizes and will not fit people of different builds.
- *A breastfeeding 'position'* allows you to breastfeed your baby in the sling or carrier – doing so takes getting used to but can provide discretion for mums who don't want to reveal all to the wider world. Ring slings, wrap slings and some pouch slings are especially suited to this.
- A model that *packs small* – so you can shove it in a bag when not using it.
- *Accessories* – babies in slings and carriers can be exposed to the elements and some models have a rain hood or sun shade or a fleecy winter cover. These can be worthwhile but you can manage without (your hands will be free for a brolly) and it isn't worth choosing a particular brand on this basis. Some carriers such as the

BabyBjorn offer dribble bibs which stop the carrier getting soaked with drool but draping a muslin cloth over the carrier will work just as well.

Parent panel tip: "It is possible to manage without a pram. I absolutely love carrying my daughter around – she's now 11 months so we use a back carrier but we've literally only ever used a pram once – we borrowed one for a wedding so she had somewhere to nap."

9

Driving

Shopping list:

✓ Group 0+ 'infant carrier' car seat

? Sun blinds

? Car seat base

? Special mirror so you can see your baby in a rear-facing seat

? Protective mat for car seat

✗ 'Baby on Board' sign

✗ Car seat footmuffs

FIRST STAGE CAR SEATS

For second stage car seats (suitable from 9kg) see page 201.

An infant car seat is one of the most important and safety-conscious baby-related purchases you'll make. Yes, it's slightly dull compared to other aspects of baby shopping, but it really is worth investing a little time in – and by that we don't just mean choosing one in a colour that matches your car upholstery. All seats sold new in the UK reach minimum safety standards but some go beyond what is 'required' performing better than others in crash tests. All our recommended brands do very well in these tests.

Once you've bought your seat, get used to fitting it in the car well before the baby's due date. Taking your first baby home from hospital can be intimidating enough without having to faff around with the car seat fitting instructions while your newborn screams the car park down.

Follow the Car Seat Golden Rules

A car seat MUST:

- *fit the car or cars it will be used in*
  Not all seats fit all cars. Before buying one, check its suitability for your make and model of car, call the manufacturer's customer care line, ask the retailer to find out, or get them to just physically check it in your car(s).

- *be installed properly*
  Even the best performers in crash tests won't be safe if they aren't fitted correctly. No matter how simple installation is, if you don't take care to read the instructions, it's easy to get it wrong. Indeed, surveys suggest between 50% and 75% of car seats are incorrectly fitted.

  Ask someone knowledgeable from the store to do a demo in your car and then to watch you doing it. Most nursery stores offer this service, although some charge a small fee, refundable on purchase of a seat. Some manufacturers' websites have helpful video instructions on fitting their car seats.

- *be bought new unless you know for sure the seat has not been in an accident, is relatively new and the manual is available.*
  Only use a second-hand seat if you *know* it hasn't been in an accident as no matter how minor, this could compromise its safety in a subsequent collision.

Car seat design improves all the time and newer models are safer than those produced more than a few years ago. Additionally, polystyrene, the main shock-absorbing component in infant carriers, degrades over time so won't perform as well when it's five years old as when new. For these reasons we thoroughly recommend buying a new seat wherever possible.

- *be the right size for your child's weight (not their age)*
  Age isn't as relevant as weight when it comes to safety. Also remember to adjust the harness every journey depending on the thickness of your baby's clothing. It's important too to adjust the height of the harness compared to your baby's shoulders from time to time – it should be at or slightly below shoulder level.

Car Seat Groups

	Faces	Weight range	Approx. age range
Group 0	rear	birth to 10kg	birth to 9 months
Group 0+	rear	birth to 13kg	birth to 15 months
Group 1	forward	9kg to 18kg	9 months to 4 years
Group 2	forward	15kg to 25kg	3 to 6 years
Group 3	forward	22kg to 36kg	6 to 12 years

A warning about infant carriers

Infants shouldn't sit in car seats for more than two hours at a time, and ideally for only two hours in total per day. Research shows newborn babies can develop breathing problems when spending long periods hunched in car seats and there are worries about the long-term effect on spinal development. Minimise use whenever possible. If you're going on a long car journey, have a break every couple of hours, taking the baby out of the seat so they can stretch and lie flat for a while.

⚠ Positioning the car seat

A rear-facing car seat should never be used in a front passenger seat with an active airbag. The safest place for it is in the middle rear seat. You can sometimes de-activate airbags but even then, using the front seat with an infant car seat should be a last resort, as the back is still safer.

About Isofix

You'll see the term Isofix a lot when car seat shopping. Whereas 'standard' car seats secure using the adult seat belt, Isofix ones plug into two fixing points under the back seat, attaching rigidly to the car chassis. In the case of infant carriers this will be via a base that stays semi-permanently attached to the car – you simply clip the carrier on and off the base.

As well as the two under-seat latches, some Isofix systems use a third fixing point called a top tether (but not all cars have these), or have a rigid support leg to enhance stability.

Since 2006 this system has been compulsory in all new cars, but some earlier models have Isofix too. Check the rear seats for the fixings (or get a car seat retailer to look for you), look in the manual, or ask the original car dealer.

Be aware that just because your car has Isofix fixings, doesn't mean all Isofix seats will fit – you'll still need to check compatibility of a particular seat for your car.

Isofix infant carriers can also be used in non-Isofix cars, secured by the regular seatbelt, but because they're more expensive (an additional £100 or so for the Isofix base), it doesn't make sense to buy one unless your main car is compatible.

Is it worth paying extra for?

The most recent crash tests suggest that Isofix seats with rigid support legs are overall the safest option and certainly perform better than seats attached using an adult seat belt.

Additionally, Isofix significantly reduces the possibility of incorrect fitting which, as mentioned above, is a very common problem that compromises safety.

Certainly, if your car has the fixings, the extra peace of mind probably makes it worth paying more for an Isofix seat and base.

Isofix: Maxi-Cosi Cabriofix with Easy Fix Base, Britax Cosytot Isofix with base, Recaro Young Profi with Isofix base.

Non-Isofix: any of the above without their bases, Bebecar Easybob, Bebe Confort Creatis

Seats with non-Isofix bases

A few manufacturers (notably Maxi-Cosi, Graco, Mamas & Papas and Chicco) offer non-Isofix bases for as little as £30 extra. As with Isofix infant carrier systems, the base stays in the car (secured by the seat belt) and the seat clicks on. With some models, you do also have to stretch the seat belt round the back of the seat to secure it each time you put the seat into the car. You should also check a non-Isofix base is firmly fitted from time to time as they can loosen.

Crucially, although these make putting the car seat in the car easier, they don't provide the additional safety benefits of Isofix. Note that each manufacturer's base will only work with their corresponding car seats, so you cannot, say, use a Maxi-Cosi base with a Graco car seat.

Verdict: potentially worthwhile if your car doesn't have Isofix and you want the convenience of just clicking the car seat onto a base.

★ *Maxi-Cosi Easybase plus Cabriofix car seat.*

When to move to a forward-facing seat

Even if your baby weighs more than 9kg, don't rush into switching to a forward facing seat – it's safer to stay rear-facing until they're 12 months *and* ideally have been sitting unaided for three months. Before this, babies' immature bones and connective tissue mean they're less able to cope with the extra stresses of a forward-facing position in a frontal collision and will be at greater risk of serious injury.

The only compelling reason to move a baby before 12 months is if they exceed the maximum weight for their rear-facing seat or if their head is above the seat top. It is not a safety issue if the baby's knees are bent or their feet touch the back seat of the car.

For these reasons, group 0+ seats are preferable to group 0 seats, since they allow babies to remain rear-facing until 13kg rather than 10kg.

Look for:

Essential:

- *Compatibility with your car* – see golden rules above.
- *Portability* – carrying the baby around in the car seat out of the car is convenient, also providing somewhere for them to sit (this should be for *short* periods only). Group 0/0+ seats are the only category that allow this – they have handles and are usually quite compact – hence the term 'infant carriers'. Some models are more cumbersome than others. Look for a lightweight seat and a comfortable handle, and avoid anything that seems physically awkward to hold.

- *Soft, easily-removable and washable covers*
- *A head hugger* – this cushion fits around a newborn's head providing extra support. They're important in that initial, wobbly-headed stage, preventing lolling about.
- *Chest and buckle pads* – padded covers that prevent the buckle and straps digging into the baby. All but the most basic models have these.

Useful:

- *Isofix* (see page 150–52).
- *A seat with a non-Isofix base* (if your car doesn't have Isofix).
- *Spare 'summer' covers* – stop the seat getting clammy in summer and can be taken off easily for washing.
- *Compatibility with a pram chassis/travel system* – many parents like to whisk the car seat out of the car straight onto a pram chassis. The idea of these so-called 'travel systems' is you're less likely to disturb a baby who has nodded off in the car. This is indeed convenient but, as we've said, infants should only be in upright car seats for short periods. Choosing a seat that can also lie flat on the pram overcomes this but they have drawbacks too (see page 154).

  Some car seats aren't compatible with any prams, some are only sold as part of a 'travel system' and a few fit on several different pram chassis. The market-leading Maxi-Cosi Cabriofix seat is the most versatile, fitting on Bugaboo, Micralite, Mountain Buggy, Phil&Teds, iCandy, Stokke and Quinny prams, amongst others. The Mamas & Papas Pro-sleep (see lie-flat seats below) also works on prams that are compatible with the Cabriofix.

  Do not be swayed into buying a car seat that doesn't fit your car properly because it goes on the pram you want – this could be dangerous.

Verdict: if you want to use a car seat on the pram often, check out lie-flat car seats (see below) made by Jane and Mamas & Papas. Otherwise, the usefulness of putting a standard seat on a pram will be limited by the fact you shouldn't let your baby sit in an upright car seat for long periods.

- *Lie-flat capability* – a few infant carriers adjust so they lie flat, some both in the car and outside of it (Jane's and Red Castle's) and some only outside of it (the Mamas & Papas Pro-Sleep).

  The lie-flat position overcomes worries about the poor positioning of babies in 'normal' car seats, and means that when you are out of the car your baby has a flat place to rest without you having to take a carrycot or similar along (although they cannot be used for overnight sleeping).

  Such seats are fantastic out of the car but there are concerns about the performance of seats in a lie-flat position in car crash tests (the Aprica Euroturn being the exception – see below). For this reason, it's best to keep them upright when the car is moving.

  Verdict: practical if you want to use the seat on a pram a lot, or out of the car. Your pram choice will be limited to compatible chassis. Keep the seat in the upright position in the car, given question marks over safety.

Mamas & Papas Pro-Sleep (compatible with various prams, although not *all Mamas & Papas models).*

Product showcase – the Aprica Euroturn is a lie-flat combination Group 0/Group 1 seat that lasts from newborn to around age three or four (18kg). Much research has gone into it and it performs well in safety tests even in the lie-flat position. Despite the fact one seat lasts through two car seat phases, given it costs around £460 for the standard model and £660 for the deluxe 'HIdx' version, it isn't a money saver compared to just buying two normal seats. It loses marks for portability too – it can't be used as an infant carrier out of the car or on a pram chassis. However, if you'll make frequent long journeys, its superior crash test performance makes it the safest option for allowing your baby to lie flat in a moving car.

- *A one-pull harness* – harnesses need adjusting frequently to ensure they remain snug according to the thickness of your baby's clothing. A 'one-pull' harness (you can tighten the straps with one pull) makes this quicker and easier.
- *Rocking base* – when using the car seat out of the car as a baby chair, a shaped base allows the seat to be rocked on the ground. This is a good way to soothe a fretful baby for a short while.
- *Sun canopy and rain cover* – if you're going to carry your baby around in the car seat out of the car or on the pram, these are worthwhile. Sun canopies are often integral to first stage seats but rain covers usually have to be bought separately.

Steer clear of:

- *Group 0+/1 combination seats* – these are a money-saving option (apart from the pricey Aprica mentioned above) as a single seat does both the infant carrier and Group 1 phases (from birth to around four). They also allow bigger, heavier babies to stay in the safer rear-facing position for longer – once they would have outgrown a Group 0+ seat.

However, they can't be used as infant carriers (they're too big and don't have a handle) which is problematic as most parents find it useful to nip into somewhere, keeping their baby in the seat (even if it is only wise to do so for short periods). Additionally, surveys suggest these seats are the ones most likely to be fitted incorrectly as they're more complicated to attach to the car. Overall by trying to be two products in one we don't find they do either job quite as well as a different seat for each phase would.

If you really want to go down this route, for fit and ease of use, the Concord Ultimax is probably the best in our opinion.

- *Car seat footmuff* – unless you'll use the car seat on a pram chassis a lot, a blanket will do just fine (but keep it over rather than under the harness) and be cheaper and more versatile. Most modern cars are pretty warm, so thick coverings are unnecessary.
- *Auto Carrycots* – these are carrycots with special attachments that fix it to the back seat. They do pass minimum safety standards but fared poorly in recent tests compared to upright infant carriers. Best avoided.

⚠ Never use a child seat that has been in an accident – even minor impacts can affect the protection it will offer and any damage might not be apparent. Your insurance company will usually cover the cost of a new one.

IN-CAR ACCESSORIES

Sun blinds – most babies get grouchy if the sun is glaring through side windows into their eyes and these are a cheap way of reducing some tears in this situation. Roller blind ones stay in place better than suction pad ones – you can choose to pull them down or roll them up as required and they're less likely to fall off and get trampled in the foot well. You can also buy a blind for the rear windscreen if you find you need it.

Clippasafe, Sunshine Kids, Safety 1st. Windowsox and Outlook Autoshades (allow you to open the car window while in place).

Baby viewing mirrors – when driving, it can be hard to check on a baby in a rear-facing seat. These large mirrors can be positioned above the baby and are useful to see their bawling/smiling face and check how they are. Most fit onto the rear head rest with adjustable straps – if you don't have rear head rests these won't be an option. You can get some that suction to the rear windscreen but they tend to be small and hard to position. Don't spend too much time gazing adoringly at your baby in the car instead of looking at the road.

This is something you can buy later on – first see how you manage without.

Easyview Mirror, Happy Mummy Mirror.

'Baby on Board' signs – you either love 'em or hate 'em. We're still debating what they're actually for. One theory is they alert emergency services to search for a baby in the event of a serious accident. We don't buy this – if the car is in such a bad way that the baby's seat and gubbins aren't visible, then we doubt that a small yellow sign stuck on with a suction pad is going to still be in place. And anyway, emergency services are trained to search the scene of an accident thoroughly – sign or no sign.

Another idea is that they're there to ask other drivers to be patient with any erratic driving. Fair enough but we doubt white van man cares if you're dealing with a screaming infant who's just vomited over the back seat. Perhaps they're simply a badge of honour to tell the world you've got a baby? If so, and that floats your boat, don't let us stop you but these really aren't a necessity.

Parent panel tip: "I always keep a bag in the car with spare nappies, wipes, and a set of Joshua's clothes. It's great for unexpected situations or times where I've forgotten something – which happens all too often with 'baby brain'."

⚠ Forgive us for repeating ourselves but this is so important that we want to reiterate the golden rules for car seats:

- Check compatibility with your car
- Install correctly – get help and advice
- Rear centre is the safest position for a car seat and a rear-facing seat should never ever go in the front if there's an airbag
- Babies should stay rear-facing as long as possible
- The harness should be checked every journey and adjusted if needed (remember also to adjust its height as your baby grows).

10

Staying safe

Shopping list

- ✓ Baby monitor*
- ✓ Childproofing items appropriate to your home
- ✓ First aid and medicine kit
- ✓ Thermometer
- ? Medicine dispensing syringe or dummy
- ? Nasal aspirator

*(unless your home is very small)

BABY MONITORS

Baby monitors allow you to keep a check on your baby when they're sleeping (or at least supposed to be) in a different room to you. You can get an idea as to whether they've drifted off (finally!)/woken-up (already?)/are crying (oh heck, not feed-time again?)

Some monitors boast extra features, from live video streaming of your baby (think 'infant Big Brother') and talkback functions, to light shows and alarms that go off if your baby stops breathing.

Do you really need one?

Our own parents managed without monitors but they've become a must-have for most modern mums and dads. If you live in anything other than the tiniest of homes and have the TV, radio or music on in the living room, you probably won't hear your baby crying in the bedroom, so a monitor will provide peace of mind.

When do you need it?

You won't need it until your baby starts sleeping in their own room so if, like most parents, you'll keep your baby close by for the first few weeks, you won't need it straight away. If you buy a monitor before the birth, keep the packaging and receipt in case, once your newborn arrives, you feel more or less protective than you expected and want a different type of monitor.

The main buying decisions:

1 Digital or analogue?

Most monitors are now digital rather than analogue with the exception of a few cheaper models and some video monitors. Analogue monitors suffer more interference from other devices than their digital counterparts. If you live in a block of flats and are buying an analogue monitor, choose one with quite a few channels to prevent cross-interference between nearby monitors and yours (it's awful to have to worry about your neighbours' monitor picking up that argument with your partner about who is more tired).

Although concerns about the safety of digital devices in the home have been dismissed by the Health Protection Agency, for extra peace of mind you could place the monitoring unit at least a metre from your baby.

★ *BT 100 or BT 150 (digital, a good range of features for the money), Tomy Walkabout Premier (a well-priced analogue monitor with up-to-date features).*

2 Video or audio?

Critics say video monitors make it easy to become a little obsessed with checking on your little one and are expensive, but they can also be genuinely useful. They allow you to take a quick look at your baby without disturbing them, so you could check whether there's an obvious cause if they're crying or whether they've nodded off yet. They're also an effective way of keeping an occasional eye on older children playing in another room.

The picture is transmitted to your TV, PC or a handheld unit, depending on the model. Avoid handheld units with a screen that's too small to see what your baby is doing.

Ensure there's an infra-red camera for when it's dark in the nursery. Until recently all video monitors used analogue technology rather than digital and so were prone to more interference. Safety 1st and Baby Essentials have now introduced digital video monitors and no doubt other manufacturers will follow soon.

★ *Baby Essentials, Summer Infant, Safety 1st*

3 Movement/breathing or standard monitor?

These have a sensor pad that sits under the cot mattress and detects movement when the baby breathes. Some monitors tick with every move, but all have an alarm that goes off if no movement is detected after a certain period, usually 20 seconds.

Some people think these monitors prey on parents' fears. There's a possibility they wouldn't warn you in time to do something if your baby stopped breathing (a choking baby could still be moving) and most medics say they're unnecessary for healthy full-term babies. They're also prone to false alarms, causing unnecessary panic (following the instructions carefully, particularly about where to position the sensor pad, helps limit these).

Despite this, some parents find movement monitors highly reassuring, especially those whose babies had breathing difficulties at birth.

Angelcare (movement and audio monitor combined), Baby Sense (the most accurate breathing monitor but it needs to be used alongside a standard monitor, so is an expensive extra).

Look for:

Essential:

- *Clarity* – you need to be able to hear your baby well without annoying interference. Note that more expensive models tend to provide a clearer signal with less interference.

Useful:

- *Dual power* – allows you to plug the monitor units into the mains or use batteries. If, like one of us, you have a house strangely prone to power cuts, or you want to wander between rooms with the monitor, a battery option is useful (check there's a low power warning light for when the batteries run out). If portability is important to you, prioritise a model that's easy to carry/has a belt clip and has a *rechargeable parent unit* (all but the most basic audio monitors have these).

- If buying an analogue monitor, check there's a *choice of channels* to help limit interference. Two or three should suffice (digital models often have many more).

- A *range* appropriate for your home and needs. Manufacturers sometimes quote both an indoor and outdoor range: 30m indoors and 100m outdoors will usually suffice but if you have a very large garden or a mansion-esque home, look for more. A lot of monitors nowadays come with a 300m outdoor range as standard.

- A *talkback function* – sometimes babies will settle back to sleep after hearing a familiar voice and a talkback function allows you to provide reassurance without necessarily going into the room. It certainly doesn't obviate the need for night feeds or the like, but can be useful, for example to persuade an early-waking toddler that the day doesn't start at 5am, without having to leave the warmth of your bed.

- *Automatic lullaby function* – means you can prompt your monitor to play soothing music when your baby makes a noise. This might or might not calm them but consider that the music could well annoy you. Potentially worthwhile for some little ones but don't worry too much if the model you want doesn't have this.

- *Light display* – these allow you to be alerted to your baby's cries by flashing lights on your receiving unit instead of sound. This probably isn't something you'll use regularly but could be helpful during a dinner party or if you make important work calls at home and don't want sudden crying to be audible. You obviously need to remember to keep an eye on the monitor otherwise it rather defeats the purpose. A few models now also offer a vibrate mode to tell you when your baby's making a noise.

Don't pay extra for:

- *Integral nursery thermometers* – some monitors have a light on the parent unit that tells you when the nursery gets too cold or hot.

Unless your baby's room is a vastly different temperature from the rest of the house, you'll have an idea of whether it's too hot or too cold without this feature.

- *Integral nightlights* – you can buy separate ones cheaply.
- *Out-of-range warning* – unnecessary, just test the range by getting someone to holler down the unit beside the baby once and check roughly where in your garden you can hear them on the parent unit.

££ : if you only want a basic monitor, check out the 'no-frills' Tomy Baby Link. Costing around £15, it's considerably cheaper than alternatives. The downside is that the parent unit only works when plugged in so it isn't very portable. Alternatively, if you'd prefer some fancier features, most people stop using their monitor after a couple of years, so it's easy to pick up decent second-hand ones.

CHILDPROOFING

The extent to which you childproof your house will depend on the nature of your home and its contents, your attitude to parenting and even, to an extent, your baby's personality.

If your house is brimming with precious nick-nacks, or particularly full of dangers, you'll need to be more rigorous. Likewise if your baby turns out to have an adventurous, inquisitive nature you'll probably need to go a step further than if they're the cautious kind.

It's hard to know where to draw the line though. Go too far and your child won't learn what they can and can't touch and will cause category five hurricane-style chaos when visiting places that aren't childproofed. Don't go far enough and obviously you risk preventable injuries (or worse) and might well spend the first few years of your child's life constantly telling them not to touch things (quite tiresome for both you and them).

Our recommended approach

- *Step 1.* Identify clear danger spots in your house and childproof them as soon as your baby shows signs of moving around. This includes anything that could cause serious injury. We also recommend fitting cabinet locks to a couple of kitchen cupboards so that you have a safe, inaccessible place to store cleaning products/that bone china dinner service you probably never use but don't want your baby to use as a missile.

  Other essentials will depend on your individual home but common problem areas include fireplaces (unless you won't use them when the baby is awake), steep steps, large expanses of glass and low cookers.

- *Step 2.* Once your baby gets more mobile, move precious items or those you don't want tipping on the floor/ripping up, out of reach. Get down on your hands and knees for an idea of what they can get to – you might notice a few things you'd missed from your adult viewpoint. Review things as your baby starts to touch loftier shelves/drawers. You might be able to avoid childproofing one or two rooms, such as a home office, by simply keeping the door shut (and locked for older ones) when the baby is around.

- Step 3. Wait and see what, if anything else, becomes problematic. Baby product companies might make you feel you need to cover the entire house in cotton wool but you don't. Some of the minor accidents that products such as table corner cushions prevent can be upsetting, but most children learn pretty quickly to be careful.

The good news is that most childproofing products are pretty cheap, the bad news is that many are rather ugly. Obviously if an item is truly necessary to keep your child safe, aesthetics are going to have to take second place for a while.

A few companies offer a childproofing service, providing a survey of dangers in your home. Childalert is the best-known provider. This is an expensive route but can be reassuring and time-saving if you want to pay to be told what you should or could do.

When do you need to do it?

Only when your baby shows signs of getting mobile. This varies but can be as early as five or six months old.

££ : Stairgates are well suited to second-hand purchase, but check fitting instructions and all screws and fixings are included.

CHILDPROOFING ESSENTIALS

Stairgates (unless you live in a one-level flat or bungalow, of course) – these prevent a baby accessing the staircase or can be used across doorways to keep little ones in or out of a room.

Most parents choose to place gates at both the top and bottom of the stairs. Check what size openings a particular gate is suitable for and whether it will fit your stairs/doorways before buying.

Types of stairgate:

1 *Fixed* – these permanently attach to the wall. They take longer to fit as they must be screwed in, so you'll have to get your drill out, but they're a sturdy, secure choice and don't have trip bars (a bar that sits across the bottom of the gate and doesn't open – it's easy to trip over

them).

2 *Pressure-fit* – easier to fit as they don't require wall-mountings or fixings, but you'll need flat walls or banisters to attach the gate to. Some have a gauge to show that the pressure is sufficiently strong but if the gate is fitted according to instructions this feature isn't necessary.

3 '*Rollerblind*' – reinforced mesh fabric that pulls across from one side of the staircase to the other where it attaches to a fixing, forming a barrier. These are currently only made by Lascal. They're especially good for awkward and wider staircases and offer the greatest flexibility. They fold away unobtrusively when not needed and don't have trip bars to fall over.

Whichever style you choose, look for a one-handed release, as you'll often be carrying your baby (or something else) when you use it.

Some models have auto-close doors which swing shut even if you forget to close them. Measure up before considering your options and don't forget any accessories you may need or extension kits if the gate you want isn't quite wide enough.

Lascal Kiddyguard (fits openings from 10cm to 130cm), Babydan ConfigureGate (works for unusual, narrow or wider stairs and doorways). Standard gates: BabyDan, Bettacare and Lindam.

Plug socket covers – blank plugs to cover socket holes, preventing small people sticking items in them. There are several different types, some easier to use than others. You will need covers even if your sockets have on/off switches. We recommend the ones where you use a pin from a plug to pull the cover off rather than those you have to prise off with your fingernails.

Drawer/cupboard locks – locking a few of your cupboards means you can keep cleaning products/your best china/knives out of reach. You needn't lock all of them. Locks can be self-adhesive or screw-in, some are visible on the outside of the cupboard or drawer and some fit on the inside.

Basic door catches are cheap and effective but need screwing in – a pain if you have a lot to fit. Multi-purpose self-adhesive locks just stick on but they sit on the outside of the cupboard so can look ugly. Some are less obtrusive than others. For double cupboards with protruding handles, slide locks are very effective. We prefer the ones that have a squeezy button in the middle and separate out rather than the sliding ones which are more obtrusive.

Sooner or later most children work out how to crack locks but by this stage hopefully they will have developed some sense of danger. Magnetic locks are the most secure – these can be particularly suited to medicine cabinets as you can only open them with the key provided. They're also invisible from the outside of the cupboard and often self-adhesive so easy to fit.

Basic door/drawer catches: Clippasafe or Safety 1st (the basic versions allow doors/drawers to open slightly, so don't prevent minor finger trappings, but your child will quickly learn to stay away. Both these companies sell anti-finger-trap versions.) BabyDan magnetic locks.

OTHER CHILDPROOFING ITEMS

Whether you need these items depends on your house – a few might be vital, others useful, some unnecessary.

Fireguards (essential if you have a fireplace you'll use when the baby is around). Look for one that attaches securely to the wall so a toddler can't pull it over, and with a top so that your little darling can't lob things into the fire.

★ *Bettacare and BabyDan.*

Window locks – these let windows be opened a little to allow air in but not far enough that a child could fall out. Whether you need them depends on the style of your windows. Some locks cannot be fitted to metal-framed or PVC double-glazed windows so check before buying.

Corner cushions for furniture – these are only really necessary if your baby is particularly clumsy and/or you have furniture with very sharp corners at toddler head level. If you need them, transparent plastic versions don't look quite as awful as white plastic ones.

DVD and video player covers – babies and toddlers love to faff with DVD and video players. These covers stop items being 'posted' into the video slot and prevent operation (although some have an integral child lock function).

Door slam stoppers – these stop small hands getting slammed in doors. There are two types, the standard white U-shaped slam stoppers that need removing when you want to close the door, and on/off stoppers that you fix to the doorpost and don't need removing.

Hob guards – prevent children reaching up to touch cooker knobs or grab pan handles (the contents could spill onto them). Some hob guards get hot enough to cause burns themselves so look for heat-resistant materials. We aren't big fans and favour keeping babies away from the cooker, either out of the room or in a playpen, or keeping pan handles away from the edge by using only the back burners. If you have a range cooker you'll find it trickier to find a solution.

Prince Lionheart guard

Cooker locks – stick-on locks to stop a baby/toddler opening low ovens. Ensure they're heat-proof. You can also buy covers for cooker knobs so that little people can't accidentally turn the hob or oven on.

Oven door guards – if you have a low oven, you can get a heat-resistant guard to stick on the oven door so that it isn't so hot to touch when it's turned on.

Fridge/freezer locks – small children love to open fridges and whilst this isn't dangerous, it can be inconvenient to have the contents emptied onto the floor, or worse still, the freezer door left open. The multi-purpose stick-on locks mentioned previously will do the same job as specific fridge locks.

Glass safety film – essential if you have expanses of glass in doors, furniture or accessible windows that aren't modern safety glass. The film sticks onto the glass so that if it breaks it won't split into shards.

Toilet locks – these stop your baby from opening the loo lid and putting their hands (or other items) into the toilet bowl or trapping fingers. Wait and see if this becomes a problem with your child. If your child goes through this phase, it probably won't last long, regardless of whether or not you invest in a lock.

Cat nets – essential for cat owners unless you can guarantee that the door to the room the baby sleeps in will always be shut, so the cat can't get in.

Blind cord winders – designed to prevent risk of strangulation from blind cords. You can manage without by just tying the cords out of reach, but then again the winders are cheap, safer and look tidier.

Playpens – these seem like a sensible way to keep babies safe if you need to answer the door, go to the loo and so forth *but* they're expensive, they take up a lot of space and the time when they are useful can be very limited. Before your baby is mobile they aren't necessary (and even in the early stages of mobility you can strap them into a bouncy chair for a short while), and once they're walking they'll probably hate being 'imprisoned' in a pen.

Pens are however a godsend if you have two children very close in age, as you can keep the older toddler from accidentally trampling on/pulling the hair of the baby without you having to watch them every second of the day. They can also help you keep toys that an older child likes playing with but that are choking hazards for a baby, away from the younger one.

Generally, instead of a playpen, we recommend using a travel cot instead. They work just as well and because they're multi-functional, offer significantly better value for money.

If you have the space, an alternative is to fit a room divider, creating a larger, childproofed area for your baby to play in.

BabyDan BabyDen (can be configured as a traditional playpen or a room divider and you can add extra panels), see also travel cota page 183.

Steer clear of:

Radiator guards – with most central heating systems you can turn the temperature down slightly so that the radiators remain effective but not so hot that burns could occur (this also helps the environment).

Cable tidies – these tuck away loose wiring from electrical appliances and lamps. You're unlikely to need them as you can almost always just hide the cables out of reach behind the appliance/furniture.

TIP: Brief relatives, carers and houseguests about child safety issues. Those who don't have small children or haven't had them recently might need reminding that, for example, they should put plug socket covers back in after using sockets.

HEALTH ITEMS

Sadly minor illnesses and injuries go with the territory with babies and toddlers. That Scouting motto 'be prepared' is a wise one here: if you keep essential medicines and first aid supplies in stock and to hand, you could save yourself a stressful dash to the all-night chemist or a frantic search for bandages.

First aid and medicine kit

You can buy a first aid kit suitable for children (and add essential medicines) or assemble your own using our list. Tell babysitters and other carers where it is. You might want to stick useful telephone numbers to the lid such as the GP's, NHS Direct and your mobile number.

We recommend including:

- infant pain reliever – Calpol, Nurofen for Children or similar (neither can be used for very new babies so check the instructions)
- antiseptic cream or spray
- tweezers and scissors
- calamine or aloe vera for sunburn and rashes

- insect bite reliever/antihistamine cream suitable for children
- bandages/dressings and plasters plus medical adhesive tape
- thermometer (see below)
- burn relief spray

Some parents also like to keep a stock of homeopathic remedies. Examples are chamomilla for teething, calendula tablets and cream for nappy rash and as an antiseptic, and arnica for bumps and bruises.

Thermometers

There are three types of thermometer suitable for taking young children's temperatures:

- *standard* – these are relatively cheap and can be used orally, under the armpit or, if you aren't squeamish, rectally. They take around 30 seconds to get a reading – it can be challenging to keep one in place with a struggling baby for that long. Avoid mercury thermometers – digital ones are easier to use.

- *forehead strips* that you hold in place until a reading comes up. They're very cheap but not terribly accurate and hard to use if a baby is wriggling around, so we don't recommend these.

- *digital in-ear/forehead* – pricier but more accurate, very quick (most provide a reading after a second or two) and can be used on babies, children and adults. Crucially, they can be used easily on a sleeping child without disturbing them.

Verdict: a digital in-ear or forehead thermometer is worth investing in as you will get years of use out of it.

Summer Infant in-ear or forehead thermometer, Babytec, Baby Essentials.

Medicine dispensers – there are two versions of these: ones that resemble mini syringes and ones that are a cross between a dummy and a mini-baby bottle. With the syringes you squirt the medicine directly into the baby's mouth and hope they don't spit it out. With the dummy-style ones, you put the medicine into a little container at the back of the teat and the baby sucks it out. Some babies who aren't used to bottles or dummies will not accept the latter type. Both versions are cheap (under £5) so it might be worth getting one of each in case one works better than the other with your baby.

Nasal aspirators – as babies cannot blow their little noses, they can get especially bunged up when they have a cold. Extracting snot from a baby's nose isn't the most delightful of tasks but these do suck nasal mucous out effectively. Choose one with a wide bulb so that you can't force it up too far and cause any damage.

Nuk, Summer Infant.

Home baby scales – certain well-known nursery retailers are selling these for a whopping £80. We can't think of a single reason why you'd need your own. Don't buy them! Normal healthy babies are weighed frequently enough by the health visitor – any more often at home and you'll risk getting hung up on the issue. Babies whose weight gain is worryingly poor should be monitored by a health professional anyway. And what's so difficult about weighing your baby on normal scales? Step on once holding them, once without, and calculate the difference.

11

Playing

Shopping list

✓ A small selection of toys

? Bouncy chair

? Baby swing

? Playnest

✗ Sit-in activity centre

✗ Walkers

TOYS

Newborns spend much of their time sleeping and feeding but as the weeks pass, the stretches when they're awake and need entertaining will lengthen. Raiding the toyshop is enormous fun but don't go overboard. Younger babies are perfectly content with a few carefully chosen items and you will probably get given plenty of toys anyway. Most older babies, meanwhile, enjoy playing with your mobile phone/car keys/pots and pans from the kitchen as much as all those expensive toys anyway.

Here are some guiding principles for choosing toys:

- expensive doesn't necessarily mean more appealing to your baby – the box the toy comes in is often of more interest.
- toys should be easy to clean – either wipe-able or washable.
- buy one or two items that attach to the car seat or pram – they won't fall into a puddle/into the car foot well which invariably leads to crying.
- accept that having at least some garish toys strewn across your house is an inevitable part of parenthood – they'll appeal to your baby even if they don't appeal to your sense of style.
- hold back from buying a few bigger items in case generous relatives want guidance on gifts to buy for junior.
- if your child becomes particularly attached to a specific small toy or teddy, buy a spare to prevent meltdowns if it gets lost.

Recommended toys for babies

Here are some of our favourite things to entertain little people during their first year:

From birth

Toys with bold black and white imagery – newborns respond better to these than to colour and many are fascinated by them.

> ★ *Manhattan Toy's Mind Shapes and car seat gallery and Tiny Love's Black and White Bumper Book.*

A musical mobile – these transfix many infants but consider that they need to be removed from the cot once babies start sitting up – as early as five months. Choose one where the interesting bits face down as your baby will be lying under it. Some are pointlessly dull from underneath.

Tiny Love Symphony in Motion Mobile (offers both movement and music and the music box is useful even once the mobile must be removed for safety reasons).

A baby gym – the bizarre name conjures up some sort of infant health club but these are simply padded mats with integral toys dangling from an arch above, sometimes with a musical function. Most babies happily lounge about on them, gazing at the dangling toys and later on trying to bat them and catch them. They're quite expensive but very worthwhile.

Tiny Love Gymini range, Whoozit Gym to Go, Baby Einstein Discover and Play.

From three months

- Baby Einstein DVDs (yes we know watching TV isn't ideal but these are lovely, purpose-designed for babies and mainly just pictures of animals and moving toys set to music. Don't be put off by the name – babies love them and they're not at all about 'hot-housing' your infant into the next Einstein).
- 'Shaky' toys and rattles.
- Brightly coloured fabric books.
- Teething rings.
- Multi-purpose soft activity toys – the best are small but packed with features to hold a baby's interest: crinkly fabrics and textures, bells, squeaky bits, baby safe mirrors, that kind of thing. They're very portable and some attach to a car seat or pram.

Whoozit Activity Spiral/Baby Whoozit.

From six months

- Toy mobile phones and keys (but they'll still try and grab yours).

- Toys with buttons to press to elicit sounds and lights.
- Bath toys.

From nine months

- Stacking cups.
- Push and/or pull-alongs.

££: larger baby toys such as activity centres and swings can keep babies entertained when you need to get on with chores but are expensive and most will only be of interest for a few months. With this is mind, borrow or buy second-hand. Such items also take up a lot of space, so hold off and see what you'll find useful and have room for.

CHAIRS AND ROCKERS

Having a few different places to put your baby when they aren't being cuddled or fed will help to keep them content. A bouncy chair or rocker is a staple of most new parents' homes – a place for short naps, for feeding during early weaning and a vantage point, letting babies get a better view of the world.

They either bounce or rock with the baby's movement and some have extras like toy bars and vibrating or music functions. They're almost all suitable from birth until six to nine months, depending on the model and the baby's weight.

As with car seats, you shouldn't leave a newborn in a baby chair for more than a couple of hours unless it reclines flat or almost flat. Certainly they aren't a great place for napping compared to a flat carrycot, Moses basket or cot.

Baby bean bags, sold as an alternative to bouncy chairs, must be designed specifically for newborns, have a harness and be firm and supportive.

Do you really need one?

A baby chair is definitely useful although not essential.

When do you need it?

Worth buying before the birth, although they should only be used for newborns for short periods if they can't be made flat or almost flat.

Types

1 *Bouncy chairs* – quite basic with a fabric seat stretched over a wire frame. The baby's movement makes the chair bounce.

2 *Rockers* – more sophisticated and usually more expensive, well-padded with several seat positions, usually including somewhat of a recline. You make these move by gently rocking them.

Look for:

Essential:

- A secure *harness.*
- A *washable or wipe-able* seat, especially if you might use it for feeding later on.

Useful:

- *A recline-able seat* – a chair that can be upright or lie flat/almost flat is preferable for longer periods of use and can double as a place for naps.
- *A rocking base that can also be fixed* – some babies are soothed by rocking, others aren't, so being able to choose is best.
- A *vibrating function* – some chairs have a vibrate function designed to settle babies. Not all babies like this though.
- A chair that *folds flat* for travel or storage.

- A *toy bar* – but ensure it detaches as it could get in your way when taking your baby in and out.
- *Carry handles* – make it easier to move the chair around.

Don't worry about:

- *Too many extras* – this chair is only going to last from birth to six months so don't spend a fortune on something very flashy.

Chicco Range (comfortable, well-priced, can lie flat), BabyBjorn Babysitter (unusually it is suitable from birth up to age two).

'Bumbos' and similar

Our parent panel are divided on these –they rank high on the list of 'wastes of money' but a few parents loved theirs. Bumbos are rubber tub chairs that support a baby at the stage where they'd quite like to sit up but can't manage it alone. They're touted as useful for early weaning but since they have to be used on the floor rather than on raised surfaces, they aren't that comfortable for the 'feeder' who has to crouch alongside.

Their window of use is also very short and worryingly some parents report that their baby could flip themselves out of theirs. The manufacturers openly state the seat is not meant to be restrictive and a baby shouldn't use it unattended.

Verdict: these aren't a worthwhile purchase given the short usage period but if you really want one, buy second-hand or borrow, and never use one on an elevated surface.

A similar product is the Bebepod, made by Prince Lionheart – it's harder plastic than the Bumbo but features a tray which can be useful and might help stop a baby flipping out.

SIT-IN ACTIVITY CENTRES

With these, the baby sits in a fabric seat surrounded by a ring featuring assorted toys and activities. They're much safer than wheeled versions known as walkers (see below). Overall, however, we still don't recommend splashing out on these as they're bulky, unattractive, expensive and only useful for a short window of time. By all means borrow one though as an extra place for your baby to play for short periods, if you have space.

PLAYNESTS

A large inflatable or cushioned ring, with toys attached. These provide extra support during the stage when a baby can't sit unaided without toppling over rather spectacularly but would like to watch the world. Later on they make a fun place to climb in and out of (perhaps from around five to ten months).

★ *Galt Playnest*

BABY SWINGS

Some parents absolutely swear by these motorised indoor swings to settle fussing or crying newborns. We aren't huge fans for the same reasons as with activity centres. Only consider one if you have a very unsettled baby and nothing else works. Again, given the cost and lack of longevity it might be better to buy second-hand or borrow.

WALKERS

There are concerns about baby walkers as they give babies a level of mobility they aren't naturally ready for and can be dangerous. The Association of Paediatric Chartered Physiotherapists warns against them as they encourage babies to walk in an unnatural tiptoe position and their use reduces the time babies spend on the floor practising body control in the natural developmental way. There is no evidence that these actually help a baby to walk earlier anyway. Steer clear.

DOOR BOUNCERS

These allow your baby to bounce around in a doorway, usually triggering giggles from said little one (although a few babies dislike them). They look fun, yes, but again The Association of Paediatric Chartered Physiotherapists isn't keen, as they encourage babies to bounce on their tiptoes and arch their back unnaturally.

TIP: Create a 'treasure basket'. Once a baby is able to pull up on things, assembling a basket of treasures for them to rummage through is a fantastic, cheap way to keep them happily occupied. Fill a large container with items of varied shapes and textures (obviously everything must be baby safe). Include wooden spoons, flannels, an old mobile phone, an egg whisk, short pieces of ribbon or fabric off-cuts – the possibilities are endless.

12

Travelling

Shopping list

- ✓ Sun cream and insect protection
- ? Travel cot
- ? Portable highchair/booster seat
- ? UV protection clothes
- ? Swimming nappies
- ? Swimming aids
- ✗ Sun protection tents/shelters

TRAVEL COTS

Travelling light is rarely possible for new parents – you're going to be dragging piles of baby paraphernalia along for the ride for the foreseeable future.

Travel cots have been particular culprits when it comes to using up that luggage allowance. Conventional models are bulky and weighty (typically around 10kg), and certainly not something you'd want to drag around whilst trekking through the Himalayas (admittedly not something most new parents contemplate). Thankfully, innovative and much more portable designs have hit the market recently, although for reasons we'll go into below, for some parents the conventional type will still be preferable.

Do you really need one?

For the first few months, you can use your carrycot or Moses basket instead (provided you have one – if not, then yes, you might need a travel cot).

After that it depends on your travel plans. Most hotels, villas and B&Bs can provide cots, obviating the need to drag your own along. If you'll stay somewhere where this won't be the case, perhaps with friends or relatives, then yes, you probably will need one.

To extract more 'value' from a travel cot, they can be used as a place for downstairs naps in the early months, or as a playpen (see page 186). A money-saving option is to club together with friends and share one, provided you won't be away at the same time.

When do you need it?

Probably not from birth. Wait and buy one if and when you need it.

Types of travel cot

1. *Conventional* – usually bulky and heavy (around 10kg) but sturdy and easy to assemble. Conventional travel cots do the 'double as a playpen' job well, as they're relatively robust and most have see-through mesh sides. Their weight and size won't be a major issue if you mainly travel by car or the cot will be left assembled at the grandparents' house. Some come with a bassinette for newborns, a changing tray or integral toys.

2. *Tent-style* – similar to tents, these are held up by poles threaded through fabric. Most can act as sun protection shelters outdoors.

They're also light and compact (some as little as 2kg) but can be tricky to put up.

3 *Pop-up* – very light (around 2kg), compact and easy to use. They pop-out of a carry bag and some have self-inflating 'air' mattresses. They're very easy to put up but take a little practice to pack away and because they aren't so sturdy (more boisterous toddlers could topple theirs) they might need to be placed between a sofa and bed or similar. For this reason they aren't ideal for use as playpens.

How to decide:

Think about the places you'll travel to and your usual mode of transport. If you'll mainly use trains, planes or coaches, then minimising weight and bulk will be wise.

Look for:

Essential:

- *Ease of use* – you can buy the best-looking, fully featured travel cot but if it requires a degree in engineering to erect, you'll be cursing it when you arrive at your destination late at night, desperate to get you and your baby to bed quickly. Check product reviews online for others' views and get a demo in-store.
- *A decent size when assembled* – if it isn't big enough for a two or three year old, it won't last until your baby can sleep in a proper bed, meaning you'd need to buy a second, larger travel cot later on. Consult the marketing literature for the cot's age range recommendation. Samsonite's pop-up models are guilty of this (the newborn version lasts until six months and even the larger one only until 18 months) and are therefore best avoided. Also be wary of square mattresses – your normal cot sheets might not fit.

Useful:

- *Lightweight* – (essential if you travel by plane or train a lot) conventional models weigh as much as 13kg, pop-ups and tent-style cots as little as 2kg. If you prefer a conventional model, try the Roomo which is around 7kg.
- *Compact size when folded up* – check to see how much luggage/ boot/cupboard space the cot takes up when it's packed away.
- *Multi-use potential* – some parents use a travel cot as a playpen when their baby gets mobile. More robust conventional models are more suitable for this than pop-ups and tents. Look for mesh sides for better visibility. Most pop-ups and tents double as UV sun protection shelters, but we don't think these are that necessary anyway (see sun protection shelters below).
- *A wheeled carrybag* – to improve portability with heavier conventional models.
- A *self-inflating mattress* – (for unconventional models) convenient and less bulky for you, more comfortable for your baby.
- *Mosquito netting:* this isn't usually included with conventional cots so you'll have to add a separate insect net where biters are a concern. Most pop-ups and tents have this as standard.
- A *bassinette* – some travel cots have a raised area for younger babies so you can get them in and out more easily without bending over the cot-side so much. These add weight and bulk and are only worthwhile if you'll use the cot a lot in the early months as they are not suitable for older babies.

Don't worry about:

- A *travel changing unit* that fits on top – just use the floor or your bed when you're away.
- *Fancy features* such as integral nightlights/ music boxes/ vibrating mattresses/ toys – none of these are necessary and add extra weight and cost.

- *A spare or thicker mattress* – travel cots tend to come with either inflatable mattresses or very thin vinyl-covered ones. These lack the comfort of standard cot mattresses but are adequate for occasional use. You can buy thicker travel mattresses but these are only worthwhile if the cot will be used very frequently in one place as they're bulky. Check with the manufacturer before adding your own mattress as this could compromise the safety of the travel cot.

Pop-ups: Bushbaby Egg, Nscessity Sun Essentials. Conventional: BabyDan (takes standard sized cot sheets), Oomo Roomo (lightweight), Graco Pack n Play. Tent: Phil and Ted

Product showcase – the Arms Reach Co-Sleeper, which we've mentioned in the 'first beds' section too. It's a fantastic bedside cot, with one side that drops down so you can sleep beside your baby without actually sharing a bed. We're mentioning it here too as it can also be used as a travel cot. It's a little heavy compared to the ideal but if you like the idea of it as a cot at home it could mean you needn't buy a travel cot.

Arms reach co-sleeper

Verdict: If you need a travel cot to do 'serious' travel with, go for a lightweight option, otherwise consider a conventional one which can double as a playpen.

PORTABLE HIGHCHAIRS AND BOOSTER SEATS

Once your baby reaches the weaning stage, you'll enter the literally murky world of the restaurant highchair. Whilst many are perfectly acceptable, some are so coated in the remnants of other babies' dinners, you'll think twice before putting your little darling in them. Taking your own portable highchair overcomes this. Even if you'd rather not take one along to restaurants, they're worthwhile for taking to friends' or relatives' houses and when you have other people's children visiting and need a second highchair.

Do you really need one?

They're actually less useful for holidays than might be expected as most hotels/restaurants/villas provide highchairs and they're an extra bit of luggage. However, ours got their money's worth of use at grandparents' houses and when other children were visiting. You could manage without but we think they're a worthwhile buy.

When do you need it?

Definitely not before the weaning stage (five to six months). Even in early weaning you can usually just spoon-feed your baby on your knee or in their pushchair.

Types:

1 *Plastic 'portable' highchair with tray* – these are plastic seats with a harness and small tray that strap onto a standard chair. If you remove the tray these double as a booster seat, for toddlers. They last the whole period when your child needs some sort of highchair and are great value (£15 to £25). They tend to be quite garish and we've put those little inverted commas around 'portable' as they're bulky and therefore unsuitable for anything other than car travel. They also have quite a few nooks and crannies for food to gather in.

> ★ *First Year, Safety First or Argos's portable plastic highchairs, or Ikea's Antlop (see main highchair section).*

2 *Fabric dining chair harness* – these loop around or over the chair back with a fabric T to hold your baby in place. They pack away very small but can get dirty, so must be machine washable. They only really work for early weaning as once a baby wants/needs to

self-feed, they don't add any height so don't help a baby reach the table. They are however very cheap (around £10) so you could move on to a booster once you reach that stage.

★ *Clippasafe Dining Chair Harness (more adaptable than others of this type).*

3 *'Clamp on' seat*/'table seat'– a fabric seat suspended from a metal ring that clamps to the table. They're relatively light and compact but must be fitted carefully to ensure safety and can be difficult to keep clean.

★ *Phil&Teds Me Too.*

4 *Booster pad* (either plastic or inflatable) – these are really glorified cushions but are very effective at allowing toddlers who no longer need strapping in better access to the table. Not suitable for younger babies given the lack of harness.

★ *Prince Lionheart booster pad.*

5 *Rigid booster seat* (usually wooden) – these strap on to a dining chair, fitting most but not all chairs, and have an integral harness. They don't have a tray so your child eats at the table. Although manufacturers of the most commonly sold version claim suitability from seven months, some parents find they aren't supportive enough for another month or two. They are however easy to clean and pack flat for holidays or restaurant trips.

★ *Handysitt, Litaf.*

6 *Inflatable seats* – these are only suitable from 12 months but probably the best suited to travelling as they the most lightweight and compact of all options.

★ *First Years Inflatable booster seat.*

Look for:

As you can see none of the available options are perfect for all age groups and situations. To decide which might suit you best, think about how you travel (and therefore how important weight and bulk are), the age of your baby when you're buying it and where you'll use it.

- *Adjustability* – check whether the seat and tray can be positioned at different heights. Will it adjust to fit all, or at least nearly all, shapes of dining chair?
- *Comfort* – support and comfort are crucial especially for a younger baby who might only just be sitting up.
- *Ease of cleaning* – as with standard highchairs, watch out for nooks and crannies and ensure materials are either machine washable or wipe-able.

Don't worry about:

- *Reclining seats.*

SUN AND INSECT PROTECTION

Sun creams and insect repellents can contain harsh chemicals so we recommend going organic where possible. Our philosophy is that if you can skip the chemicals without compromising on effectiveness, and often without spending extra, why wouldn't you?

Suncreams

You probably won't need suncream for your baby initially, as they shouldn't be in direct sunlight during their first few months. Choose a gentle formulation suitable for sensitive baby skin. There are several ranges of organic suncream for children, some of which are available in supermarkets and high street stores.

Organic Children or Lavera's lotions, Dr Hauschka, Sunsense (not organic but low on chemicals and high on protection and good for children with eczema or sensitive skin).

Insect repellents

Insect repellents can contain very strong chemicals and are often labelled as unsuitable for young children. There's particular concern about the use of the chemical DEET. Hunt around and you can find natural insect repellents that can be used on young children. Mosi-Guard is a natural formulation, fairly widely available and fine for children. Even when using insect repellent it's wise to keep your baby's skin covered when most at risk.

If your baby does get bitten, a soothing witch hazel or aloe vera preparation is an effective natural remedy.

Sun protection clothing

Sun protection clothes save you from constantly slathering your child's entire body with suncream, which can be tricky if they're wriggly and uncooperative (and many little ones are when it comes to this task).

You can probably make do with just one or two of these outfits for holidays as they dry rapidly. Look out for fabric that's breathable and, if going for the suits, something that's easy to put on and remove. These garments can be pricey but your child will live in them on beach holidays. Most baby clothes stores or departments will have some in stock in summer.

Don't forget a decent wide-brimmed or legionnaires-style hat too.

★ *Platypus, Sun Essentials.*

UV shelters

These tents are designed to block harmful UV rays on the beach or in the garden. We don't think they're worth buying because younger babies can be kept in the shade with a pram sunshade or beach umbrella and older ones are unlikely to want to stay in the shelter – especially with the lure of sand to play on.

If you do buy one, also bear in mind studies have questioned whether some are as effective at blocking UV as they suggest, so do err on the side of caution. Also, look for good ventilation to prevent overheating.

Shelta UV Sun Tent.

SWIMMING

Swimming nappies

If your holiday will involve dips in the pool, swimming nappies are essential. Unlike normal nappies, they don't swell up and weigh your baby down. Choose between disposable and washable versions. If you go for washables, you'll need to think about laundry arrangements if they do get soiled.

Disposable: Huggies Little Swimmers. Reusable: Bambino Mio, Kushies or Splashabout.

Swimming aids and clothing

There are now far better swimming aids than those uncomfortable to put on arm bands most of us endured as children. Modern roll-on versions go on much easier without annoying the wearer's little arms. An alternative is a buoyancy jacket – these are rather more expensive but worth investing in if you'll go swimming regularly.

For younger babies, swim seats are cheap and effective although some little ones prefer to be carried in your arms at least initially.

Neoprene baby wraps insulate a baby in water and can be the difference between your baby loving the water and hating it.

Zoggs roll ons, Splashabout Swim Wraps, Floaties Swimseats.

13

No longer a baby

Shopping list

✓ Potty or toilet trainer seat

✓ Other toilet training items – pants, wipes, disinfectant

✓ Second stage car seat

✓ Toddler or single bed plus bedding

? Bed guard/rail

? Back carrier

? Hip seat

From the announcement of your impending parenthood onwards, countless well-wishers have probably advised you to 'enjoy every minute – they grow up so fast'. Like many clichés it's a true and indeed savvy one. Before you know it, that tiny, mewing infant is a walking, talking, tantrumming little person and yep, you guessed it, needs a whole new raft of products.

As a minimum, there'll be a forward-facing car seat, a big boy/girl bed and a stack of potty training stuff. Thankfully these items don't all need to be bought at once, so there's much less of a shopping frenzy involved than there was around the time of the birth.

POTTY TRAINING KIT

You'd think that after a couple of years of dealing with nappy contents, you'd be blasé about pee and poo. However, the prospect of potty training is fairly universally dreaded by parents. Our job isn't to advise on the timing, tricks and techniques involved – there is plenty of information elsewhere on that. But might we say that in our experience waiting until your toddler is 'ready' will make it much less of an ordeal. The right time to cast those nappies aside is a very individual thing, so don't worry about trying to compete with baby X who was 'dry' at 18 months.

Essentials:

- **A potty or toilet training seat** (or both). See page 196. If you have a large house buy more than one so there's always one nearby if your child needs to go in a hurry.
- **'Big kid' pants** – let your toddler choose a design they find appealing so they 'buy into' the idea of wearing them. Purchasing a size larger makes them easier for your toddler to pull up and down. Some people like to use training pants for extra protection in the early stages. We favour reusable ones over disposables as the latter are too much like nappies and don't allow a child to feel wet.
- **Packs of wipes/cloths and disinfectant spray** for cleaning up accidents. A natural disinfectant spray, one made with tea tree oil, is good to have around.
- **A waterproof sheet/pad** – place one under a child's 'un-nappied' bum in the early days of training to save the sofa/car seat from a soaking. These don't have to be plasticky (see mattress protectors page 111) and a good tip is to reuse your old carrycot or crib

mattress protector. Once you tackle night-time training a good idea is , once again, to get a flat, non-plasticky mattress protector and use it on top of your child's fitted sheet to speed up middle of the night bed changes.

- **A step stool** – makes for easier access to the sink for hand-washing and for climbing onto the loo seat (it also makes them feel more secure when on the loo if their feet can touch the ground).

- **A travel potty or toilet seat adapter** might also be worthwhile. The 'Potette' is a small folding potty that uses disposable liners so you easily dispose of the contents if you're out. The 'Toodleloo' meanwhile, is a foldaway toilet seat adapter which is great for use on loos away from home.

Potties and trainer seats

Do you really need them?

You need a potty or a seat, not necessarily both because some children go straight to using the loo, skipping the potty stage. However, most start with a potty and graduate to the loo later, using a toilet trainer seat to make it appropriately sized for a toddler's little bottom. You can either buy a separate trainer seat (the padded ones with handles are good) or replace your main toilet seat with one that has both an adult-sized seat and a child-sized one. This also means there is always a child seat available for visiting children even when yours no longer need it.

When do you need it?

It depends on when you begin potty-training – most children are nappy-free in the daytime anywhere between two and three. Babies in washable nappies often train earlier as they are more aware of feeling 'wet'. It's worth sitting a baby on a potty from as young as 12 months to get them used to it though, even if training in earnest starts later on.

Look for:

Essential:

- *Comfort* – if the potty or seat isn't comfortable your little one isn't going to want to stay on it.
- *A splash-guard* for boys – potties and toilet trainer seats should have a raised front to help contain 'spraying' by little boys.

Useful:

- With toilet trainer seats, look for *handles and padding* to help your toddler feel more secure and comfy.
- A *high back* on a potty could make a reluctant toddler feel more secure and comfortable.

Don't bother with:

- Gimmicks – musical potties aren't usually necessary.

BabyBjorn Potty Chair (high backed, removable inner bowl for easy cleaning and splashguard at the front – bulky so you might need a second, smaller potty when going out). Bibs and Stuff padded toilet trainer (with handles, padded seat and splash guard).

'BIG KID' BEDS AND BEDDING

At some stage you'll need to set your little one free of their cot bars and let them sleep in an open bed. If your child has a cot-bed, this will merely mean taking the sides off, so you can delay buying a full single bed until about age five or six. If they have a standard cot though, you'll probably need to move them to a bed anytime between the age of two or three.

The triggers for moving to a bed are usually when your child tries to climb out, risking injuring themselves (although you can help prevent such escapades by using a sleeping bag back to front so they can't undo it), when they physically outgrow the cot or when they are night-time potty trained.

Toddler beds are available that are smaller and lower to the ground, but we favour going straight to a full-sized single bed. Toddler bed frames are relatively cheap but once you add in a mattress and potentially smaller bedding, they aren't great value given you'll also have to buy a single bed later on anyway. If you're worried about your toddler falling out of a higher bed, you can fit a bed rail to help prevent this.

Bedding

Toddlers don't actually *need* pillows and indeed back care experts would argue it is healthier to delay introducing one for as long as possible. When you do give your toddler a pillow, washable versions will be better than standard ones.

A duvet, meanwhile, will be lighter and more practical than blankets and sheets. Go for a lower tog rating than you would for adults – 4 togs should suffice for toddlers and you can always add a blanket on top. Again, go for one that's machine washable and get a spare in case of accidents or for when the main one is in the wash.

When choosing duvet covers, it's tempting to go with your toddler's current favourite 'kiddy character' but consider that you'll probably want the bedding to do for several years, whilst your little one's penchant for Postman Pat might last mere months. Plain bedding and a few 'character' accessories might be a wiser choice.

Product showcase – an innovation from the makers of Grobag sleeping bags is the Grobag 'first duvet and bedding set', sold in cot-bed or single bed sizes. Its clever design means the duvet cover securely attaches to the integral fitted bottom sheet using a zip on both sides. This makes it easy for a child to get into bed, but, once zipped up, they can't fall out (so there's no need to bother with bed rails). The pillowcase is also attached to the sheet, keeping it snugly in place. The designs are not too garish and the fabric high quality.

★ *first bedding set from Grobag*

TODDLER CARRIERS/BACK PACKS

Whilst front carriers and slings can be wonderful for younger babies, they can strain your back and shoulders once your child gets heavier. Switching to a back carrier can allow you to continue enjoying the convenience of carrying your child long into their toddler years.

Types:

Conventional back carriers are similar to framed rucksacks, with shoulder and waist straps – junior sits where the bag would go. They're normally suitable from around six months when a baby is sitting up and has stronger neck muscles. They're relatively straightforward to use especially if they're freestanding on the ground, making it easier to load your child into and get onto your back. However, they are very bulky and won't pack into a holdall for a holiday or day out.

Soft frameless carriers such as the Ergo and Patapum aren't quite so practical for all-day use but pack much smaller. Unless you're regular walkers, we favour these over conventional models. They're fantastic for use around the shops instead of a buggy, or to give a toddler who mainly walks an occasional break. They can be tricky to use at first –

getting your child onto your back is a bit of a juggling act, so get someone else to help the first few times.

Look for:

Generally, many of the considerations in our baby slings and carriers chapter apply for back carriers too, so before shopping it might be worth re-reading them. Here are some key issues for back carriers.

Essential:

- Something that's *easy to use* and get your toddler into. As with front carriers, try and get a demo in the shop or look for one online. If you're buying a conventional backpack look for one that can *stand alone on the floor* so you can put your toddler into it more easily.
- A carrier that's *lightweight* so as not to add to the overall weight you have to drag around.
- *Well-padded shoulder straps* to prevent digging in.
- *Adjustable straps* – especially if more than one person will use it.

Useful:

- *Leg stirrups* – somewhere for your little one's legs to go, aiding weight distribution for you and comfort for them.
- A *sun/rain canopy* – normally only available on conventional models.
- A *sleep hood* – this means that if your child falls asleep in the carrier, their head will be supported rather than lolling around.
- *Pockets* for stowing other stuff so you needn't carry a bag too.
- Something that *packs away small* when not in use. Conventional back carriers will inevitably be somewhat bulky.

For hiking or all-day trips, the Macpac Possum, Bushbaby, Little Life or Kelty ranges. For briefer everyday or holiday use, the Ergo or Patapum (both can also be used on the front).

Product showcase – if you only need to carry your toddler for short periods, the Hippychick Hipseat can be easier on your body than using your arms, spreading weight onto your hips, and also allowing you to keep an arm free. They're easy to use, strapping around your waist like a large belt with a platform seat that your little one perches on upon your hip. A hip seat isn't a replacement for a buggy or back carrier but can be helpful on occasions where perhaps a toddler gets too tired during a walk, or to carry a younger child a short distance without the hassle of getting the buggy out of the car. They can be used from around six months to three years. Note though that, although better for your spine than normal carrying, they're not ideal if you have a bad back. If this applies to you it might be worth borrowing a friend's to see if you find it a comfortable way to carry your child. If you do want to get one, given use will probably only be occasional, it's worth trying to pick one up second-hand.

SECOND STAGE/GROUP 1 CAR SEATS

Most parents are eager to move their child into a forward-facing car seat as early as possible, many switching as soon as their child reaches the minimum weight for a Group 1 seat, rather than when they've really outgrown the rear-facing one. Why? Well, everyone thinks their baby will be happier facing forward watching the world. And whilst generally this is true, what those happy front-facing babies don't realise is that they're actually much safer facing rearwards in the event of a collision.

So when is the best time to change to a front-facing Group 1 seat?

We thoroughly recommend you delay the switch for as long as you can.

- Don't do it because your baby's feet are pushed against the car's back seat.
- Wait until they've been sitting up for a minimum of three months, as this indicates they are physically able to deal with the extra stresses of a collision in a front facing seat.
- Wait until they're closer to the maximum weight (13kg for a 0+ seat) for their rear-facing seat than the minimum weight (9kg) for the front facer.
- *But* do move them if their head is protruding over the top of the Group 0/0+ seat. If they outgrow the seat in height but have not reached the minimum weight for a group 1 seat, you'll have no choice but to get a combination group 0/1 seat (see page 154). Not an ideal scenario but the only safe one.

Do you really need one?

Yes, it's the law if your baby will be travelling in a car.

When do you need it?

See page 201 – definitely not before your baby is nine months old *and* weighs more than 9kg but ideally later.

Look for:

Really many of the same things as when you were buying that first infant car seat (see page 154).

- *The seat must fit your car* and others it will be used in regularly.
- *Easy to remove, washable seat covers.*
- *A one-pull harness.*
- Some newer models have a *harness tension indicator* to show

whether the harness has been pulled sufficiently tight to be safe.

- *A recline option* – whilst an infant carrier will be in a semi-reclined position all the time, a Group 1 seat will be more upright. A recline option will make the seat more comfortable if your little one needs to nap in the car.

Issues that were relevant for your infant seat but aren't so here are compatibility with a pram chassis (front facing seats can't be used in this way), and portability (you won't be using the new seat as a carrier out of the car).

When it comes to **Isofix**, the same pros and cons apply as before and obviously you need to have a car with the relevant fixings. Overall, an Isofix seat will be considerably more expensive and heavier but will be safer. Whilst infant carriers attach to the Isofix fixings via a separate base, Group 1 seats, in general, have integral fixings so a separate base won't be needed.

Non-Isofix: Bebe Confort Axiss (rotates making it easier to get your child in and out), Maxi-Cosi Tobi, Isofix: Maxi-Cosi Priorifix, Britax Duo Plus, Britax Explora Isofix, Recaro Young Expert with Isofix base (this uses the same base as the Recaro infant car seat so one base works for both stages).

Combination seats

You can buy a single 'combination car seat' to cover both the Group 1 and 2 phases (from nine months to around six years) and sometimes the Group 3 period (ages six to 12) too. These seem like money-savers but there are concerns that they're not as safe as standard Group 1 car seats for younger children if they do not have a five-point harness, using the adult seatbelt to restrain a child in the Group 1 age range instead.

If a combination seat appeals – perhaps so the grandparents only need buy one seat for use to age 12 in their car, the Britax Evolva 123 is a solid choice.

Car seats beyond age three

Don't forget the law states your child should remain in a suitable car restraint until they are either 135cm tall or reach their 12th birthday. For this stage, high back boosters offer much greater protection, especially in a side-on impact, than booster cushions.

14

The definitive baby shopping list

CLOTHING

✓ Sleepsuits (6 x newborn size, 6 x 0-3 months)

✓ Short-sleeved bodysuits (6-8 x newborn, 6-8 x 0-3 months)

✓ 2 cardigans in 0-3 months (lightweight for summer, medium-weight for winter)

✓ 2 hats

✓ 4 pairs of socks

✓ 2 pairs of scratch mitts

✓ 2-3 bibs

✓ 2 pairs of mittens (winter babies only)

? 2-3 sleepgowns

CHANGING (nappies)

✓ Nappies

✓ Cotton wool pads and/or wipes

✓ Nappy rash cream

✓ Lidded nappy bin and two laundry nets (if using washables)

✓ Changing bag or equivalent

✓ Muslin cloths or towelling squares

✓ Nappy sacks

? Nappy disposal unit

? Changing mat

BATHING

✓ Soft towel solely for your baby's use

✓ Baby nail clippers or scissors

✓ Flannel or sponge

? Baby bath

? Newborn bath support

? Bath ring (for use from around six months)

? Bath thermometer

? Toiletries

FEEDING

✓ Two feeding bottles (six if you plan to mainly bottle-feed)

✓ Three breastfeeding bras

✓ Breast pads

✓ Nipple cream

✓ Steriliser

✓ Highchair

✓ Weaning spoons and bowls

✓ Training cups

? Breast pump (*essential if you develop mastitis or engorgement)

? Breastmilk storage containers/bags

? Formula milk (essential if bottle-feeding from birth)

? Formula dispenser

? Breastfeeding pillow

? Nipple shields

? Baby food blender

SLEEPING – FIRST BEDS AND THE NURSERY

✓ Cot/cot-bed plus mattress

✓ Storage – drawers, wardrobe or both

✓ A comfortable chair for feeding

? Smaller first bed such as a Moses basket, plus mattress

? Changing unit

? Blackout curtains or blinds

? Nursery decoration

SLEEPING – BEDDING

✓ Bedding (if using a smaller first bed you will need two sets in different sizes):

 3 or 4 fitted sheets

 2 mattress protectors

 2 or 3 sleeping bags OR 4 blankets and 3 or 4 flat top sheets

? Swaddling wrap

? Cot separator (for twins only)

? Sleep positioners

? Baby sheepskin

? Cat net (essential if you have a cat)

? Cot bumpers

? Coverlets

WALKING (PUSHCHAIRS, SLINGS AND CARRIERS)

✓ Pram/buggy with a lie-flat seat or carrycot (unless using a sling/ carrier all the time)

✓ Raincover

? Footmuff

? Sunshade and insect net (for summer/holidays)

? Buggyweights

? Sling/carrier

DRIVING

✓ Group 0+ 'infant carrier' car seat

? Sun blinds

? Car seat base

? Special mirror so you can see your baby in a rear-facing seat

? Protective mat for car seat

? 'Baby on Board' sign

STAYING SAFE

✓ Baby monitor*

✓ Childproofing items appropriate to your home

✓ First aid and medicine kit

✓ Thermometer

? Medicine dispensing syringe or dummy

? Nasal aspirator

*(unless your home is very small)

PLAYING

✓ A small selection of toys

? Bouncy chair

? Baby swing

? Playnest

TRAVELLING

✓ Suncream and insect protection

? Travel cot

? Portable highchair/booster seat

? UV protection clothes

? Swimming nappies

? Swimming aids

NO LONGER A BABY

✓ Potty or toilet trainer seat

✓ Other toilet training items – pants, wipes, disinfectant

✓ Second stage car seat

✓ Toddler or single bed plus bedding

? Bed guard/rail

? Back carrier

? Hip seat

Index